THE NEW TECHNICAL TRADER

WILEY FINANCE EDITIONS

FINANCIAL STATEMENT ANALYSIS
Martin S. Fridson

DYNAMIC ASSET ALLOCATION
David A. Hammer

INTERMARKET TECHNICAL ANALYSIS
John J. Murphy

INVESTING IN INTANGIBLE ASSETS
Russell L. Parr

FORECASTING FINANCIAL MARKETS
Tony Plummer

PORTFOLIO MANAGEMENT FORMULAS
Ralph Vince

TRADING AND INVESTING IN BOND OPTIONS
M. Anthony Wong

THE COMPLETE GUIDE TO CONVERTIBLE SECURITIES
WORLDWIDE
Laura A. Zubalake

MANAGED FUTURES IN THE INSTITUTIONAL PORTFOLIO
Charles B. Epstein, Editor

ANALYZING AND FORECASTING FUTURES PRICES
Anthony F. Herbst

CHAOS AND ORDER IN THE CAPITAL MARKETS
Edgar E. Peters

INSIDE THE FINANCIAL FUTURES MARKETS, 3RD EDITION
Mark J. Powers and Mark G. Castelino

RELATIVE DIVIDEND YIELD
Anthony E. Spare

SELLING SHORT
Joseph A. Walker

TREASURY OPERATIONS AND THE FOREIGN EXCHANGE
CHALLENGE
Dimitris N. Chorafas

THE FOREIGN EXCHANGE AND MONEY MARKETS GUIDE
Julian Walmsley

CORPORATE FINANCIAL RISK MANAGEMENT
Diane B. Wunnicke, David R. Wilson, Brooke Wunnicke

MONEY MANAGEMENT STRATEGIES FOR FUTURES TRADERS
Nauzer J. Balsara

THE MATHEMATICS OF MONEY MANAGEMENT
Ralph Vince

THE NEW TECHNOLOGY OF FINANCIAL MANAGEMENT
Dimitris N. Chorafas

THE DAY TRADER'S MANUAL
William F. Eng

OPTION MARKET MAKING
Allen J. Baird

TRADING FOR A LIVING
Dr. Alexander Elder

CORPORATE FINANCIAL DISTRESS AND BANKRUPTCY, SECOND
EDITION
Edward I. Altman

FIXED-INCOME ARBITRAGE
M. Anthony Wong

TRADING APPLICATIONS OF JAPANESE CANDLESTICK CHARTING
Gary S. Wagner and Brad L. Matheny

FRACTAL MARKET ANALYSIS: APPLYING CHAOS THEORY TO
INVESTMENT AND ECONOMICS
Edgar E. Peters

UNDERSTANDING SWAPS
John F. Marshall and Kenneth R. Kapner

GENETIC ALGORITHMS AND INVESTMENT STRATEGIES
Richard J. Bauer, Jr.

THE NEW TECHNICAL TRADER
Tushar S. Chande and Stanley Kroll

THE NEW
TECHNICAL TRADER
Boost Your Profit by Plugging
into the Latest Indicators

Tushar S. Chande and Stanley Kroll

JOHN WILEY & SONS, INC.
New York • Chichester • Brisbane • Toronto • Singapore

Library of Congress Cataloging-in-Publication Data:

Chande, Tushar S., 1958–
    The New Technical Trader : Boost Your Profit by Plugging
    into the Latest Indicators / Tushar S. Chande and Stanley
    Kroll.
        p.   cm. — (Wiley finance editions)
    Includes bibliographical references and index.
    ISBN 0-471-59780-5
    1. Investment analysis—Data processing. 2. Futures
    market—Data processing. I. Kroll, Stanley. II. Title.
    III. Series.
    HG4529.C45 1994
    332.6'0285—dc20   93-36663
                                                              CIP

Printed in the United States of America

10 9 8 7 6 5 4 3 2 1

To my other coauthors
Vidya, Ravi, and Aroon

TC

Preface

This is a book about new technical indicators. You will find these indicators useful because, although markets have changed, technical indicators have not. The analytical "thinkware" has lagged behind trading hardware and software.

This is an intermediate-level book in technical analysis. We have assumed that you have a working knowledge of trading, technical analysis, computers, spreadsheets, and technical analysis software.

You can group the indicators in this book into two broad areas: new methods of price analysis and risk control. A brief description of the new material follows:

- Linear regression analysis quantifies trends and projects prices for developing a game plan.
- VIDYA is a variable-length exponential moving average that is indexed to volatility or momentum.
- Qstick is a quantitative candlestick that gives you a number to look at rather than a pattern to ponder.
- New momentum oscillators are derivatives of the relative strength index that help overcome its limitations.
- Market thrust is an improvement on the Arms index.

- Maximum favorable excursion analyzes profitability of your losing trades; it is useful for aggressively managing new trades.
- Volatility-based stop is an advancing stop from volatility.
- Typical trade profile shows price-time evolution of typical a trade from your model; it is useful for open trade management.
- Price targets are used to formulate a specific trade plan.

We'll explain our indicators in detail, using tutorials and practical examples, giving specific rules for trading futures, indices, stocks, or mutual funds. The last chapter shows how to combine these indicators into unique and powerful trading systems. We hope to stimulate your efforts to adapt our new indicators to your trading style, which will give you an analytical edge in today's tough markets.

Acknowledgments

Modern technical analysis software is at the heart of this book. We want to thank Bill Cruz of Omega Research, Miami, FL, for giving us System Writer Plus and SuperCharts. We liked the power and simplicity of both programs. We also want to thank Allan McNichol and Equis International, Salt Lake City, UT, for a test copy of their Technician software. The market thrust material was developed from their data. Many of the charts were compiled based on data supplied by Commodity Systems, Inc., of Boca Raton, FL. We also used data from Technical Tools, Inc., of Los Altos, CA, using their Continuous Contractor software.

No book is ever complete without multiple drafts of the manuscript. We want to thank Nauzer Balsara for his comments on an early version of this text. We want to thank Thom Hartle, editor of *Technical Analysis of Stocks and Commodities* magazine, for reviewing an early draft. Jack Hutson, publisher of *Stocks & Commodities*, gave us permission to use the articles upon which this book is based.

Our thanks to Myles Thompson, our editor at John Wiley & Sons, Inc., for his guidance and support. We also want to thank the reviewers at John Wiley for sharing their insights.

Contents

1 An Abundance of Indicators   1

The Significant Failure Rate of Indicators, 1
Similarities Among Popular Indicators, 3
New Indicators for Price Analysis, 10
New Ideas for Risk Control, 12
Putting It All Together, 14

2 Linear Regression Analysis   19

How to Use Linear Regression Analysis, 19
Case in Point: The Coffee Market and Linear Regression, 25
Case in Point: Intel Corporation and Trendiness with r^2, 29
Case in Point: T-Bond Forecasts for the Next Trading Day, 34
Developing a Forecast Oscillator, 40
Summary, 42

3 The Variable Index Dynamic Average   49

The Simple Moving Average and Its Responsiveness, 50
Trading Strategies, 54

Case in Point: VIDYA and T-Bond Market Analysis, 55
Summary, 62
Tutorial: Spreadsheets for VIDYA, 63

4 Qstick: The Quantitative Candlestick   73

The Basics of Candlestick Analysis, 73
Qstick: Intraday Momentum Indicator, 75
Case in Point: Qstick and Crash of 1987, 77
Qstick and Momentum, 79
Quantifying Candlestick Shadows, 82
Case in Point: Analyzing Three Stocks with Qstick, 85
Summary, 90
Tutorial on Qstick, 90

5 New Momentum Oscillators   93

Chande Momentum Oscillator, 94
Tutorial: Defining RSI, 119
Stochastic RSI Oscillator, 124
Variable Length Dynamic Momentum Index, 134
Summary, 141

6 Market Thrust and Thrust Oscillator   143

Market Thrust and Thrust Oscillator, 145
Summary, 159

7 Controlling Risk: The Key to Profitability   161

Estimating Risk on New Positions, 163
Developing a Trade Template, 169
Anticipating Prices for a Risk Control Plan, 172
Practical Issues in Risk Control, 175
Controlling "Invisible" Risks, 178

8 How to Use This Book   181

A CMO-Driven VIDYA Trading System, 181
Market Rotation, 189

Bibliography   195

Index   199

THE NEW TECHNICAL TRADER

1
An Abundance of Indicators

There is no shortage of indicators in technical analysis. We know an indicator is a mathematical formula for analyzing price action based on prices, or volume, or both. One popular software package has over 50 built-in indicators. The sheer number of price-based indicators suggests the question: Are any redundant? In fact, there are strong similarities between price-based indicators, and using them simultaneously creates redundancy.

THE SIGNIFICANT FAILURE RATE OF INDICATORS

Even the best indicator does not work 100 percent of the time; hence, using indicators is a game of percentages. Since each indicator has a significant failure rate, traders have developed many indicators to analyze prices, the random nature of price changes being one reason why indicators fail. Therefore, traders use multiple indicators to confirm the signal of one indicator with another. They believe that the consensus of indicators is more likely to be correct.

Can you recognize the stock, commodity or index shown in Figure 1.1? Following well-known principles of technical analysis, note that prices topped at A, and began a downtrend in January and February. The downtrend accelerated when support failed at the 26.00 level. Prices made a rounded bottom in late March, bouncing off B on one final selling climax.

Prices then rose in a tight channel to the 26.00 level. Prior support became the new resistance, and prices entered a trading range. The resistance at the 26.00 level is marked C, and is roughly at a 50 percent retracement of the decline from A to B. You can observe the hammer and doji formations near the bottom, the spinning tops in the trading range, and the hanging man formation near the top.

Don't be disappointed if you didn't recognize the fictitious price chart in Figure 1.1. We developed those realistic looking

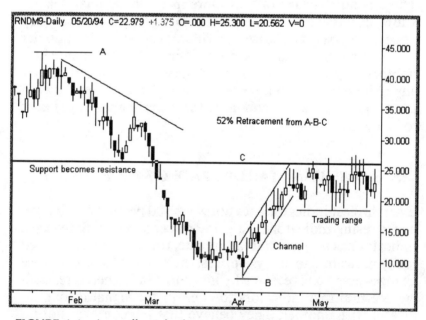

FIGURE 1.1 A candlestick chart of randomly generated prices.

prices using a random number generator and a spreadsheet. Nevertheless, many features shown there are found on real price charts, such as support and resistance, rounded bottoms, and 50 percent retracements, although there is no reason to find those features on a chart of randomly generated prices. Some elements of technical analysis may work simply by pure chance; hence, their failure rate remains uncertain.

We usually do not know the true reasons for price changes. We could speculate that prices were overbought, or oversold, or at resistance, or in support. It is easy to develop a plausible explanation for market action after the fact. But, you must use objective price analysis to develop the consistent decision making necessary to trade with random price movements. You should also use strict risk control to cope with unexpected price movements.

The new material in this book should help your efforts. Our new indicators for price analysis and risk control will help you overcome key limitations of existing ones. Ultimately, they could boost your profitability.

SIMILARITIES AMONG POPULAR INDICATORS

You can find brief descriptions of different indicators in various books or software manuals, but you will rarely see the derivation of these indicators or an analysis that describes what is new or different about an indicator. We think it's reasonable to ask: What do the indicators mean? Here we will examine several popular indicators based on price and show how similar they are.

These popular indicators measure price momentum in one form or another: directional movement system, momentum, relative strength index (RSI), stochastic oscillator and commodity channel index (CCI). The William's %R is a complement of the stochastic oscillator; hence, it has the same information as the stochastic oscillator. The price-rate-of-change is, by definition, a momentum calculation, and we will not discuss it separately. The price oscillator, though smoothed, is also similar to momentum.

Charting the Similarities

You may wish to verify visually the similarities among these indicators using the price action of Philip Morris (MO) stock. In Figure 1.2 you can see the 14-day momentum, relative strength index, and stochastic oscillator for MO from October, 1992 through July, 1993. The three indicators look alike, particularly near significant turning points. Note that momentum has an unbounded scale. On the other hand, both RSI and the stochastic oscillator vary from 0 to 100.

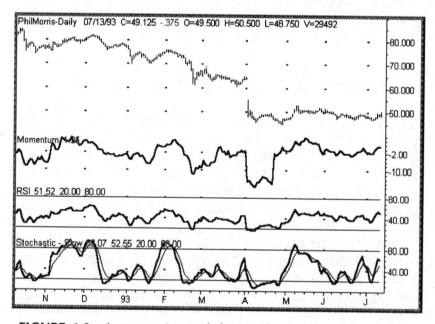

FIGURE 1.2 A comparison of the 14-day momentum, relative strength index, and stochastic oscillator for Philip Morris stock.

Figure 1.3 shows the similarity between the 14-day RSI and the 14-day plus directional index indicator for MO. Observe how both indicators peak and bottom together. Figure 1.4 compares the 14-day commodity channel index (CCI) with the 14-day stochastic oscillator. These two indicators are also similar in appearance, and their turning points occur at about the same time.

The CCI is compared with a price oscillator in Figure 1.5. The price oscillator is the difference between today's close and a 14-day simple moving average of the close. The CCI behaves like this oscillator, though it has different scaling factor; both track momentum (see Figure 1.6).

There are other examples of using the difference in moving averages to measure momentum. For example, notice how the 14-day momentum to the popular moving average con-

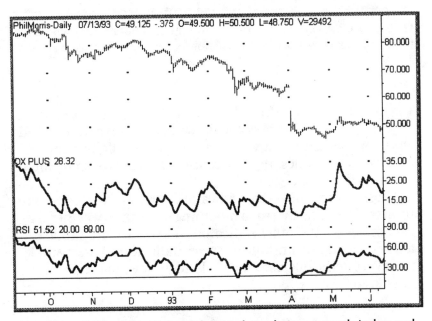

FIGURE 1.3   A comparison of the 14-day relative strength index and the plus directional movement (DX+) for Philip Morris stock.

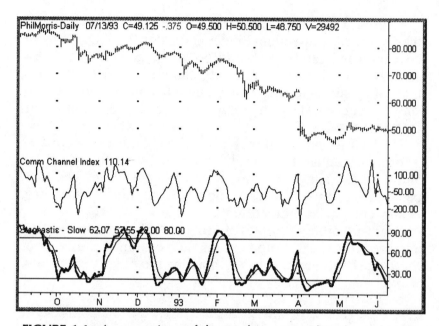

FIGURE 1.4 A comparison of the 14-day commodity channel index to the 14-day slow stochastic oscillator for the same data as in Figures 1.2 and 1.3.

vergence-divergence (MACD) indicator bottomed together in Figure 1.7. The MACD is the difference between 12-day and 26-day exponential moving averages of the daily close. As momentum declines, the difference between two exponential averages declines also.

These figures show that indicators derived from prices are similar. The differences in smoothing determine whether they lead or lag behind other indicators. There also are subtle differences in the definition of these indicators. For example, not every indicator uses the daily high, low, and close in its calculations.

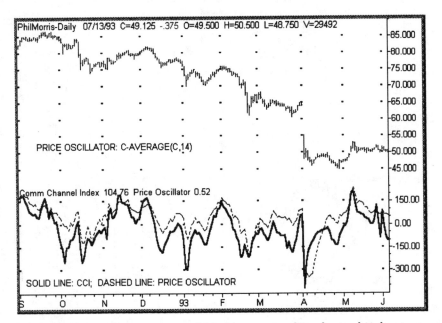

FIGURE 1.5 A comparison of 14-day commodity channel index to a price oscillator for Philip Morris stock.

Correlation Among Indicators

A quantitative way to show the similarities between indicators is to calculate the statistical correlations between them. To do this, we use linear regression analysis on indicator pairs. The similarity is quantified using the coefficient of determination (denoted by r^2). If two indicators move together, they are perfectly correlated, and the value of r^2 will be 1.0. The value of r^2 will be 0 if they move randomly compared with one another. The higher the value of r^2, the less random the relationship between the two indicators.

The statistical correlations between these indicators was calculated using the Commodity Systems, Inc. (CSI) 39 Perpetual contract for deutsche mark futures over a recent 150-day period. We have listed the coefficient of determination

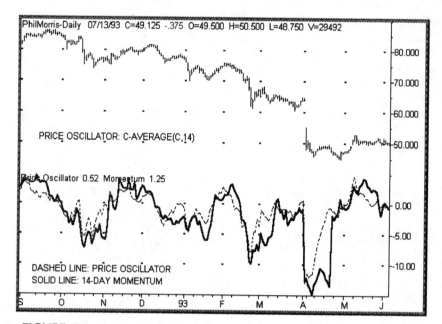

FIGURE 1.6 A comparison of the 14-day momentum and the price oscillator in Figure 1.5 for Philip Morris stock.

(r^2) values in Table 1.1. All the indicators are correlated, thus the r^2 values approach 1; therefore, using these indicators simultaneously does not provide additional information. The high correlation is not surprising, since the indicators are based on daily prices. Subtle differences in their definition and scaling affect the measured correlation.

The purpose of this discussion is to point out the unavoidable similarities between price-based indicators. Each indicator provides a different perspective on price action. Your trading style and analytical approach will determine whether you use one indicator or another. However, using all these indicators together does not yield additional information.

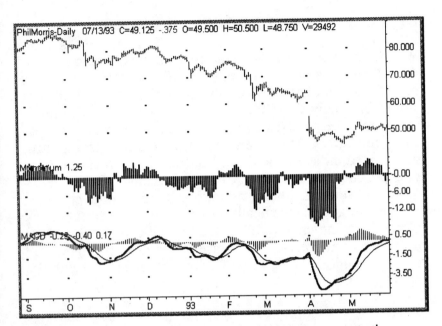

FIGURE 1.7   A comparison of the 14-day price momentum to the moving average convergence-divergence indicator for Philip Morris stock.

Table 1.1   Statistical Correlation Using 14-Day Calculations for Deutsche Mark CSI #39 Perpetual Contract

Indicator Pair	r^2
Momentum vs. RSI	0.93
Momentum vs. Stochastics	0.78
Momentum vs. CMO	0.93
RSI vs. Stochastics	0.77
RSI vs. Plus Directional Index	0.78
CMO vs. ADX	0.82

CMO = Chande Momentum Oscillator
ADX = Wilder's Average Directional Index
RSI = Wilder's Relative Strength Index
CSI = Commodity Systems, Inc.
r^2 = 1, perfect correlation
r^2 = 0, no correlation

NEW INDICATORS FOR PRICE ANALYSIS

Why then, are new methods of price analysis necessary? You need them to give you an edge in the markets. Obviously, indicators that overcome specific limitations of existing ones would be highly desirable. In fact, insights from new indicators may be gained without a strong correlation with existing indicators. These new indicators fall into two groups: price-based indicators and risk control tools. Most of the indicators can be used on any market, whether futures, commodities, stocks, indices, or mutual funds, although one—market thrust—is specifically designed to analyze the stock market. The indicators address many problems, including improved pattern recognition, variable indicator length, and price projection. Thus, these flexible indicators will fulfill a variety of needs.

Linear Regression Analysis

Wouldn't you trade better if you could peek into the future? Unlike most technical indicators, linear regression analysis can develop price forecasts for the next trading day. The forecasts are not meant to provide the precise high or low of the next day; rather, they provide some guidance for developing a specific plan for trading. This method also allows you to quantify the strength of the linear trend in the data, and is helpful in following the long-term trend.

Variable Length Moving Averages

You know that moving averages use a fixed number of days of previous data. This is a significant limitation, since the most profitable length for the average changes without notice. Wouldn't it be helpful to use a moving average that adjusts its "length" automatically, based on price action? The variable length dynamic index (VIDYA) does just that. It is a modified exponential moving average that adapts to market volatility, increasing its length when prices trade in a narrow range, and shortening it when prices move rapidly. VIDYA slows down when prices are quiet, and speeds up when prices make their move. You can adjust the responsiveness, or dynamic range, to suit your trading style. The dynamic range is the range of effective lengths that VIDYA can use, say, from 3 to 30 days. VIDYA is therefore a flexible moving average, which is a significant improvement on fixed-length moving averages.

Qstick: Quantitative Candlestick

Japanese analysts believe that the candlestick method of price pattern recognition has predictive value, helping the trader react faster than when using a moving average. However, interpreting patterns is still a subjective process. Qstick extracts the essence of the candlestick approach by taking a moving average of the daily difference between the closing and the opening price. Qstick, the quantified candlestick, gives you a number to evaluate, rather than a pattern to ponder, reducing the subjectivity in using candlesticks.

Momentum Oscillators

The Chande momentum oscillator (CMO) is a pure momentum oscillator. The stochRSI combines the powerful ideas of relative strength and a range location oscillator. They will often show price extremes that the relative strength index (RSI) will not, helping to overcome its limitations.

The CMO can show net momentum at a glance, and can be combined with VIDYA to form a dynamic average keyed to market momentum. The stochRSI quickly shows price extremes and momentum swing failures because it reaches new lows and highs faster than the RSI itself. You thus can combine the two popular ways to use RSI into a single indicator.

We complete our oscillator group by extending the idea behind VIDYA to RSI, defining the dynamic momentum index. DMI also adjusts its own length using market volatility; thus, you do not have to specify the number of days in the calculations. DMI often leads RSI into overbought or oversold territory by many days, a useful feature most traders could exploit.

Stock Market Thrust and Thrust Oscillator

Finally, we present a new way to analyze stock market advance decline data. Up thrust (down thrust) is the product of the number of advancing (declining) issues and the up volume (down volume). Market thrust is the daily difference between up thrust and down thrust, and can be cumulated or smoothed without distortions, a significant improvement on the trader's index or TRIN. TRIN has an unbounded scale on days with large volume in declining issues. We overcome this limitation by defining a thrust oscillator that provides a bounded range for relative volume flows on up and down days. The thrust oscillator may be visualized as a volume oscillator or an advance/decline oscillator, useful because major market bottoms tend to occur when the 21-day smoothed thrust oscillator is at or below −0.30.

NEW IDEAS FOR RISK CONTROL

Along with the new indicators for price analysis, we also introduce the following ideas for risk control.

Maximum Favorable Excursion

The maximum favorable excursion (MFE) analyzes losing trades from a trading system to help manage open trades more aggressively during the first few days of the trade. For example, when the maximum profit is less than some amount, the stops should be closer than when the profit is greater than some other amount.

Typical Trade Profile

Another new way to manage an open trade is the idea of typical trade profile, which shows the evolution of prices in time for trades from a given model. Here we analyze daily equity of all the trades from a model to derive the "signature" of trade equity changes in time. This price-time profile can be used to close out trades that do not follow the usual path. Thus, you can catch losers early and cash out of fast-rising winners using these profiles. They provide an objective way to manage the open trades.

Contingency Planning

Contingency planning should also be part of a risk control strategy. We look at the practical issue of developing a game plan, suggesting a way to project the possible price range for the next day using absolute momentum. These numbers then provide targets for a "what if?" simulation, a proactive approach to trade planning. This will help you preplace your orders and trade more mechanically. In our discussion we also touch upon practical issues of trailing stops, trading tactics, portfolio selection, and asset allocation. Some of these ideas may already be familiar to you.

PUTTING IT ALL TOGETHER

There are many new ideas in this book that you can integrate into your trading style. The ideas are flexible and powerful, so you can easily adapt them to your analytical approach and planning process. The more ideas you can integrate, the more you can boost your trading profitability.

Tutorial: Reasons for Similarities Among Indicators

This tutorial will clarify the reasons for the similarities among the indicators shown in Figures 1.2 through 1.7. We begin by defining momentum as the difference between today's close (day 0) and the close x days ago.

$$\text{momentum} = C_0 - C_x \qquad (1.1)$$

For our purposes we will use $x = 14$ days. Momentum can be positive or negative, so we also define the absolute value of momentum.

$$|\text{momentum}| = |C_0 - C_x| \qquad (1.2)$$

A common practice is to separate momentum into days when prices close up and days when prices close down.

$$
\begin{aligned}
\text{up-day momentum} &= C_0 - C_1 \text{ if } C_0 > C_1 \\
&= 0 \text{ otherwise} \\
\text{down-day momentum} &= C_1 - C_0 \text{ if } C_0 < C_1 \\
&= 0 \text{ otherwise}
\end{aligned}
\qquad (1.3)
$$

This definition gives positive numbers for both up-day and down-day momentum. We can now sum up-day momentum and down-day momentum over 14 days.

S_u = 14-day sum of up-day momentum   (1.4)
S_d = 14-day sum of down-day momentum

We now write RSI using these definitions that ignore the smoothing scheme in RSI calculations for the sake of simplicity.

$$\text{momentum} = (S_u - S_d)$$
$$RSI = 100\ (S_u/(S_u + S_d)) \qquad (1.5)$$

This shows that momentum and RSI are closely related because they both involve the term S_u. Thus, the high correlation is to be expected. The unsmoothed stochastic oscillator is defined using the close, highest high (HH), and lowest low (LL) over a 14-day period. It shows where the close is within its range over 14 days.

$$\text{stochastic} = \frac{(C_0 - LL_{14})}{(HH_{14} - LL_{14})} \qquad (1.6)$$

The close tends to be near the high or low of the day when markets make new highs or lows. You can check many price charts to verify this observation. Hence, highest high can be replaced by the highest close (HC). This is usually a good approximation over the calculation period. Similarly, the lowest low is replaced by the lowest close (LC).

$$\text{stochastic} = \frac{(C_0 - LC_{14})}{(HC_{14} - LC_{14})} \qquad (1.7)$$

This now takes on the appearance of a momentum calculation, where the number of days can vary between today and x days. Assume that the lowest close was 14 days ago. The numerator would then be $(C_0 - C_{14})$, a momentum calculation. Thus, we expect to see a broad similarity between stochastic oscillator and momentum. There will be some lags because of the smoothing scheme in stochastic calculations.

When a market is moving strongly up or down, the price range tends to lie primarily beyond the high or low of the previous day. Suppose the market makes new highs for the move 14 days in a row. Assume also that each day the market closes at the high. Here the unsmoothed RSI = 100 since S_d = 0. The plus directional movement (DX+) also would be 100 (before smoothing) since the largest part of each day's action (directional movement) was equal to the daily true range. The broad similarity between RSI and DX+ follows from their definitions (see Figure 1.3). Smoothing schemes and actual definitions account for the differences.

The commodity channel index starts by defining M, the mean price of each day, as the average of the daily high, low, and close. Next, a 14 day moving average of the mean price (M_{avg}) is used to calculate a deviation D.

$$D = M - M_{avg} \tag{1.8}$$

A scaling factor is developed by taking a 14-day moving average of the absolute deviation ($|D|_{14}$). The 14-day CCI is then the ratio of D and its scaling factor.

$$CCI = D / (0.015 * |D|_{14}) \tag{1.9}$$

Note that the numerator D determines the sign and change in CCI. We can replace the mean price by the daily close C. This provides an excellent approximation more than 95 percent of the time. Hence, the deviation D now becomes a momentum-like calculation, where we take the difference between today's close and its 14-day simple moving average (C_{avg}):

$$CCI = (C_0 - C_{avg}) / (0.015 * |(C - C_{avg})|_{14}) \tag{1.10}$$

The CCI then reduces to a price oscillator, with one-day

and 14-day moving averages (see Figure 1.5). Price oscillators also measure momentum, as you can see in Figures 1.6 and 1.7. There are differences in scaling caused by the denominator of each indicator. There are also differences in the smoothing process within each indicator. However, we can expect broad similarities, particularly at key turning points. This also explains the similarity between momentum and the moving average convergence-divergence (MACD) indicator, since MACD is a price oscillator using exponential moving averages.

Tutorial: Generating Random Prices

We used an Excel (version 3.0) spreadsheet with a random number generator to build a price pattern. For our purpose, we assume that the random number generator is perfect. The following tutorial illustrates the process of generating ten days of data. You can follow the same process to generate more days as needed.

We first generate 10 random numbers that are either +1 or −1 to signify an up day or down day. We use the following rule:

(if(rand( ) > rand( ), 1, −1)).

The built-in Excel function rand( ) returns a random number between 0 and 1 inclusive. This rule generates two different random numbers; if the first number is greater than the second, today's price is greater than yesterday's price (+1). Otherwise, today's price is lower than yesterday's (−1).

To start the series, we assume that the close of the first day is 40.00. This could be the price of a stock or the price of a commodity in cents per pound or cents per gallon. We also assume that today's high or low can be no more than 2 cents above or below the close. We thus generate a random number between 0 and 2 and add it to the close to get the high. Similarly, we generate another random number between 0 and 2 and subtract it from the close to get the low. The rules are as follows:

today's high $=$ today's close $+$ rand( ) * 2

today's low $=$ today's close $-$ rand( ) * 2

today's close $=$ yesterday's close $+$ rand( )*2*($+1$ or -1)

The Excel function rand( )*2 generates a random number between 0 and 2 inclusive. For day 2, we generate a random number between 0 and 2, multiply it by either $+1$ or -1 as determined before, and add it to the previous close. Next, we find two more random numbers to compute the high and low. We continue the process for ten periods. You can add rand( )*3 to increase the range of price action.

2
Linear Regression Analysis

Linear regression analysis is a well known method of data analysis. However, not all technical analysts use it routinely. Therefore, we will approach this material from a user's point of view, rather than attempting a mathematically rigorous application of the linear regression process. The technical analyst must cope with uncertainties using every indicator that is available, and any imperfections in the application of this method must be weighed against the usefulness of the resultant information. You'll see that there are several ways to use the results that will add value to your analysis.

HOW TO USE LINEAR REGRESSION ANALYSIS

You can visually determine from a bar chart if prices are trending, and use the mathematics of the linear regression method to fit the "best" line to a series of prices. This method uses the formula of least squares to find the best fitting line. This calculation gives us the slope and intercept of the "best-fit" line, as well as the strength of the linear trend. In this chapter, you'll discover how to trade with the slope and trend strength.

Using the equation of the best-fit line, you can estimate values of the possible prices for the next trading day. The idea is not to predict the precise high or low for the next day, although you could occasionally come quite close; it is instead to have price targets that can be used to develop a game plan for trading. You can then trade objectively within the heat of battle.

The Linear Regression Method

The linear regression method solves the following equation:

$$y = m * x + C. \tag{2.1}$$

Here x is the independent variable, y is the dependent variable, m is the slope, and C is a constant intercept. You can imagine a plot along the x and y axes of the two variables. This equation describes their relationship in a quantitative form.

The output of the regression calculations gives values for m and C. We also get the coefficient of determination, denoted by r^2. Refer to the tutorial at the end of this chapter to see why r^2 measures the relative trend strength.

We like to use five days of closing data for short-term trading using regression analysis. You may wish, however, to experiment with the number of days used in the calculations, as well as try the daily high and low prices for making forecasts.

Sample Calculations

Let's look at a sample calculation using the closing prices of a recent gold futures contract. Assuming time as the independent variable and price as the dependent variable, enter the values in a spreadsheet. (Refer to Table 2.1 during the following discussion.)

In Table 2.1, we want to fit a straight line to five days of daily closes of the gold contract. Hence, under x, the independent variable (column A), is simply the days from 1 through 5. The dependent variable shown as y (column B), is the daily close of the gold futures contract.

We will square each of the daily variable values and write them in the next two columns (C and D). Thus, the line for day 5 shows that the square of 5 is 25 (5 × 5) and the square of 388.20 is 150,699.20. The last column, E, is the product of each pair of dependent and independent variables.

The value for day 5 is 1,941 (5 × 388.2). The sum of each of the five daily values is calculated in its respective column.

In Table 2.1, we define three other terms used in the cal-

Table 2.1 Linear Regression Calculations Using Daily Close of August, 1993 Gold Contract

	A x	B y	C x-squared	D y-squared	E xy
	1.00	378.10	1.00	142959.61	378.10
	2.00	376.10	4.00	141451.21	752.20
	3.00	379.50	9.00	144020.25	1138.50
	4.00	379.20	16.00	143792.64	1516.80
	5.00	388.20	25.00	150699.24	1941.00
Sum	15.00	1901.10	55.00	722922.95	5726.60

n = number of days in the calculations = 5
q_1 = (5726.6 − ((15 * 1901.1) / 5)) = 23.3
q_2 = (55 − ((15 * 15) / 5)) = 10
q_3 = (722922.95 − ((1901.1 * 1901.1) / 5)) = 86.71
slope = q_1 / q_3 = 0.1 * (5726.6 − (3 * 1901.1)) = 2.33
intercept = ((0.2 * 1901.1) − (3 * 2.33)) = 373.23
coefficient of determination (r^2) = (q_1 * q_1) / (q_2 * q_3) = 0.626
day-6 forecast close = ((6 * 2.33) + 373.23) = 387.21
actual close = 386.70

culations, q_1, q_2, and q_3, which are computed using the totals in the various columns and the number of data points. You can find the slope and intercept of the 5-day regression from the following equations:

slope(5 day) = 0.1*(sum of product − 3*sum of y values),
intercept = 0.2*sum of y values − 3*slope.   (2.2)

In Table 2.1 the sum of the product is in column E and the sum of y values is in column B. We can also find the slope using q^1 and q^2. We get the forecast by substituting the slope and the intercept into the regression equation and using the value 6 for x, the independent variable. The coefficient of determination, r^2, was 0.626, showing a statistically significant trend. Note that the 5-day trend was up and the best-fit line was rising $2.33 per day over the calculation period.

Graphs of the Output

In Figure 2.1, note how the dotted best-fit line smooths out the variations in daily data, showing the upward trend in prices. In Figure 2.2 we step the regression line one day forward to find the regression forecast. In our example, prices retreated to close slightly below the day-6 forecast: at 386.70 instead of 387.21. The forecast is simply a "point estimate" of the daily close. We can use variation in the data to calculate a range of values for the closing price. Then actual close could lie within a band above and below the point estimate. Nevertheless, the point estimate is usually sufficient to develop a game plan for trading.

Outputs: Slope and r^2

The first output of a linear regression analysis is the slope of the trend line. The slope is positive when prices are rising

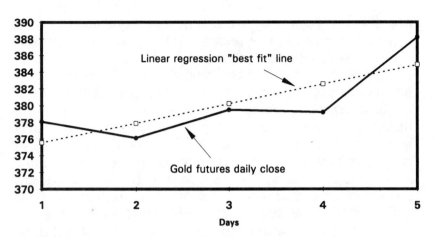

FIGURE 2.1 An example of linear regression calculations using the daily close of the August, 1993 Comex Gold futures contract. The solid line joins the daily closing prices.

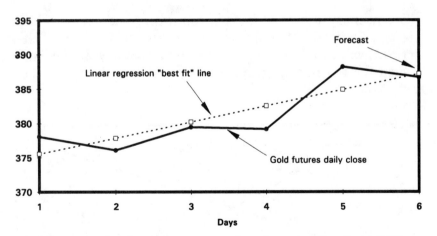

FIGURE 2.2 The day-6 closing price forecast using the "best-fit" linear regression line.

and negative when they are falling. The slope measures the expected change in price per unit of time, which, when converted into dollars per contract or share, indicates if the market is making big or small moves. The slope converted into dollars is a useful filter for trading or ignoring markets.

Linear regression analysis also gives us the strength of the linear relationship, denoted by r^2, the coefficient of determination. It is a quick measure of the trendiness in the data, ranging from 0 to 1. If there is no trend, that is, random price action, the r^2 value will be close to 0. A perfect linear trend gives a value of 1. Figure 2.3 shows two simulated sets of data: a random set and another with an exact linear trend. The r^2 value is close to 0 for the random set, and is 1.0 for the exact linear trend.

Using r^2

The primary use of r^2 is as a confirming indicator. It is a lagging indicator that shows the strength of the trend. The critical value of r^2 depends on the number of days in the data: when the r^2 value is greater than the critical value, a statis-

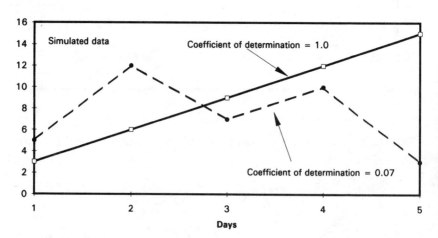

FIGURE 2.3 Simulated data showing trending and trendless data.

tically significant trend exists. For a 10-, 20-, 30- or 50-day regression, the critical values you can use are 0.40, 0.20, 0.13, and 0.08 respectively. (You can find details of these calculations in the tutorial section on linear regression later in this chapter.) The slope of the regression will tell you the direction of the trend. You can then put on positions with the trend if you wish.

Using Both Slope and r^2

You should use the slope and the r^2 values together. For example, a strong trend with a small slope may not interest the short-term trader. A moderate value of the slope, with only a weak trend in the data, may be a warning that the trend is changing. Hence, the slope and the strength of the regression are valuable inputs into a trading model. High values of the slope occur when the market is trending strongly. As the trend weakens, both the slope and r^2 will head toward 0.

In order to trade with the significant trend, simply check if the slope is positive or negative. You could open a long position when the slope first becomes significantly positive. Conversely, you could open a short position when the slope is significantly negative. You also will then see the slope make a peak (positive or negative) and turn toward 0. At this point, you may choose to take profits, tighten your stops, or take an antitrend position. The market may take a long and slow trip back to 0, in which case, an antitrend position would be unprofitable. Hence, there is a variety of trend-following and antitrending strategies possible using linear regression analysis.

CASE IN POINT: THE COFFEE MARKET AND LINEAR REGRESSION

We can illustrate these ideas using the Commodity Systems, Inc., (CSI) Perpetual contract for the coffee futures market.

Figure 2.4 gives an overview of the #39 Perpetual contract daily close for coffee. Coffee bottomed in August and September, 1992, and rose steadily into the middle of December, 1992. The coffee market was choppy as it formed a top, then collapsed in late January. Coffee rebounded strongly from an oversold condition, fell again, and then entered a brief sideways period.

We begin by arbitrarily choosing 15 days as the time period for linear regression calculations. Figure 2.5 shows the slope of the coffee data from 08/03/92 to 03/23/93. Overlaid on the slope is the coefficient of determination, r^2. You will notice that r^2 approaches 0 as the slope changes sign. Notice that high values of slope coexist with high values of r^2: this is often true for trending markets. When the trend is changing, the slope is also changing signs, and r^2 approaches 0.

Since there are trends within trends, the length of your regression calculations will influence what you see. The slopes for the coffee contract over 7-day and 15-day intervals are shown in Figure 2.6. The volatility of the coffee market can be seen by the variations in the slope of the 7-day regression.

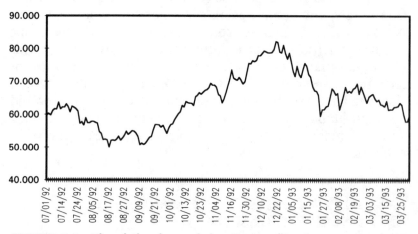

FIGURE 2.4 The daily close of the Commodity Systems, Inc. #39 Perpetual contract for the coffee futures prices.

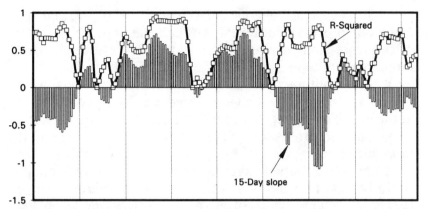

FIGURE 2.5   The 15-day slope and r^2 from a linear regression analysis of the CSI data in Figure 2.4 for coffee.

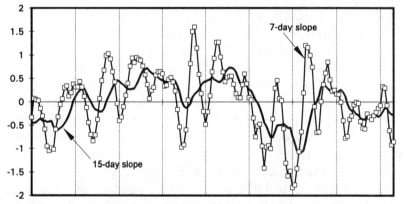

FIGURE 2.6   A comparison of the 15-day and 7-day slopes for the coffee data in Figure 2.4.

The 15-day regression slope is less volatile, showing that the regression process smooths the data considerably as the length of the regression increases. The shorter regression changed directions and signs more often, producing more trades. However, the amplitude of the move, and hence the profits, were not the same for each change in direction. Thus, your choice of the length of the regression will influence both your trading frequency and profits. In volatile markets, a shorter length is more effective.

In our coffee market example, one simple trading strategy could be based on the observation that high values of slope coexist with high values of r^2. You could go long when the slope is positive and r^2 is above 0.20, showing a statistically significant trend. You could close the long when the slope was no longer statistically significant (r^2 below 0.20). This approach would take you long at the end of September, and close you out in the dip in mid-November. You would go long again nine days later, and close out the long at the end of December. Then, you would go short in the first week of January, and close out the short in mid-February. Thus, you could catch the major moves with this strategy.

Figure 2.6 also shows how a countertrend strategy may be carried out. Using the 7-day slope, values above +1 and below −1 signal market extremes. You should be prepared to take an opposite position as the slope exceeds these limits. Then, you could wait for the slope to turn down or up before placing your trades.

You can experiment with regressions of different lengths. You also should test the models over four to five years of data to obtain reliable estimates of overbought and oversold regions for a countertrend strategy. There is no assurance that future prices will follow precisely the same pattern. Hence, you may wish to use two or more regression lengths in your analysis.

CASE IN POINT: INTEL CORPORATION AND TRENDINESS WITH r²

The linear regression r^2 is an alternative to other measures of trendiness such as the average directional index (ADX) or the vertical horizontal filter (VHF). Let's compare these indicators using Metastock software version 3.5.

We will use daily data for Intel Corporation (INTC) from 01/01/91 to 12/31/92 to make our comparison. This time span includes periods when Intel showed many different price patterns: a broad trading band, and strong up- and downtrends. Here are the Metastock formulas for smoothed r^2 and VHF. (Please refer to J. Welles Wilder's book in the Bibliography for a detailed discussion of ADX.)

smoothed r^2 = mov(pwr(corr(cum(1),c,14,0),2)*100,14,s)
smoothed VHF = 100*(mov(vhf(c,14),14,s))   (2.3)

The ADX, smoothed VHF and smoothed r^2 are in broad agreement. In Figure 2.7 we show a smoothed r^2 that is a 14-day simple moving average of 14-day r^2. Low values imply an imminent change in trend; high values show price extremes. The low values in 1991 led to tradeable trends in Intel. Observe how the smoothed r^2 peaked in 01/92 before the actual high in February. This indicator showed a falling trend (loss of momentum) even as prices moved upslowly in October, 1992.

In Figure 2.8 we have a smoothed VHF, that is, a 14-day simple moving average of a 14-day VHF. We multiplied the smoothed VHF by 100 to produce numbers on the same scale (0 to 100) as the other two indicators. Observe the broad similarities to the smoothed r^2 shown in Figure 2.7. The smoothed r^2 declines to lower values than the smoothed VHF.

Then, in Figure 2.9, we have the 14-day ADX showing the trend. Observe the similarities to Figures 2.7 and 2.8. The ADX stayed flat for most of this period except for the year-end rallies. Notice how the ADX declined in October-

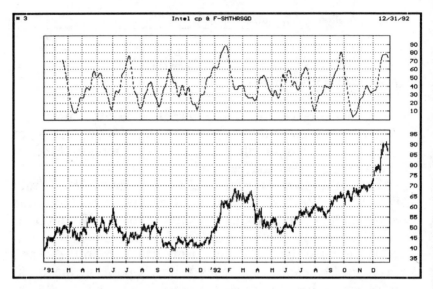

FIGURE 2.7 A 14-day simple moving average of the 14-day r² used as a measure of trendiness in the price of Intel stock.

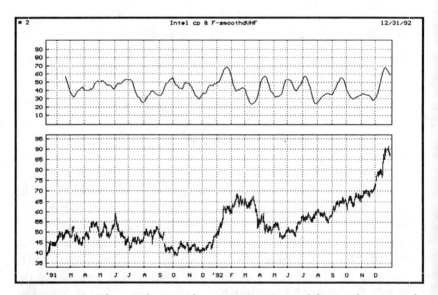

FIGURE 2.8 The 14-day simple moving average of the 14-day vertical horizontal filter used as a measure of trendiness in Intel stock.

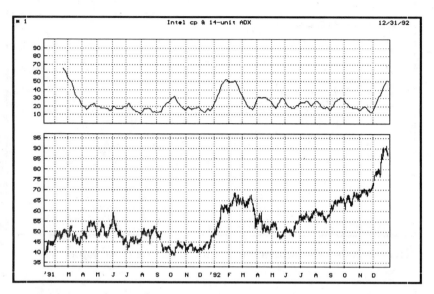

FIGURE 2.9 The 14-day average directional index used as a measure of trendiness in Intel stock.

December, 1992, even as prices moved slowly higher. The ADX had smaller swings than either the smoothed r² or the smoothed VHF.

A more direct comparison between the smoothed r² and the smoothed VHF is shown in Figure 2.10; a comparison between smoothed r² and ADX is shown in Figure 2.11. Notice that the two indicators move in unison at key turning points.

All three measures of trendiness move up as trends emerge. Hence, they move up even when prices are falling. They also usually decline during trendless periods. The smoothed r² and smoothed VHF move in unison at key turning points. But, the smoothed r² is more sensitive than the ADX, often staying at higher levels even as the ADX declines. This sensitivity demonstrates the contrast, since a declining ADX implies no trend, whereas high values of smoothed r² shows a persistent trend.

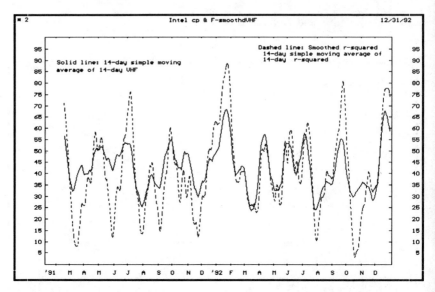

FIGURE 2.10 The superimposed smoothed r² and smoothed VHF for Intel.

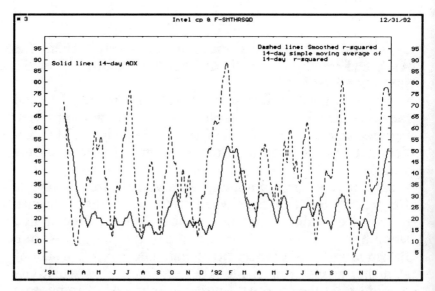

FIGURE 2.11 The superimposed smoothed r² and average directional index for Intel.

A Detailed Comparison: r², ADX, and VHF

In 1991, Intel was in a trading range between 38 and 60. The trading range narrowed to approximately 40–45 during most of October through December of 1991. It broke out of this range in the rally sparked by interest rate cuts on December 20 that year.

The 14-day ADX stayed flat below 25 from April through September (see Figure 2.9). It rallied briefly that month during a short sell-off, and quieted down again during the tight trading range. It rose with the rally from December, 1991 through February, 1992. It then declined and stayed range-bound for the rest of 1992, even as Intel moved steadily upward, only responding to the breakout above 70 in December.

Thus, the ADX rises when there are strong moves in the stock. It often declines during a tradeable downward move in prices, and it does not react well when prices rise unevenly. For example, the 14-day ADX declined in October and November, 1992, while prices rose choppily from 62 to 70.

The smoothed r² is more responsive to price changes, as you can see in Figure 2.11. Note how it moved up faster and sooner than the equivalent ADX in November and December, 1991, and again in mid-October, 1992. It peaked simultaneously with the ADX, pegging the imminent trend change in June, 1993, as Intel neared 55, and sold off sharply into July. It was a tradeable short from 55 to about 42. From this you can see, the smoothed r² has interesting properties as a measure of trendiness.

Adam White, a contributing editor to the *Technical Traders Bulletin*, proposed the vertical horizontal filter (VHF) to measure trendiness. VHF compares the range between the high and the low to the average absolute daily momentum. White does not explicitly discuss using it in a smoothed form. VHF is usually used with 28 days in the calculations. However, we find it more interesting to use a shorter time period with smoothing to isolate the underlying trend.

The smoothed 14-day VHF is similar to the smoothed r²

(see Figure 2.10). Both can go up even as prices move down. Since you can use the slope for direction, the combination of slope and smoothed r^2 provides both the direction and strength of the trend. The smoothed r^2 shows an imminent trend change by falling below 0.1. This happens even when the smoothed VHF remains at high values, giving the smoothed r^2 an edge.

A Common Weakness

All three measures of trendiness show a common weakness. After prices make a quick move (up or down) and then briefly reverse direction, the trendiness measures begin to decline, and will keep falling (suggesting no trend) even if prices later resume their initial direction. Thus, they often show a loss of momentum rather than an actual change in the major trend. The main reason for this weakness is that we are using a fixed number of days for these calculations. We get a different view of the underlying trend as we change the period of the calculations. So, there is some ambiguity about determining trendiness, since the number of days in the calculations influences the results.

CASE IN POINT: T-BOND FORECASTS
FOR THE NEXT TRADING DAY

We can use linear regression analysis to develop a regression forecast for the next trading day. First, we develop linear regressions separately for the high, low, and close. Then, we substitute the values of slope and intercept into the linear regression equation and calculate the new value for the next trading day. Consequently, we can forecast the high, low, and close. Statisticians call this approach the point forecast. We also can develop a confidence interval for the forecast high, low, and close. This interval is the range within which we can expect the actual values to fall with, say, 95 percent confidence.

Strategies

We don't expect to forecast precisely the actual high, low, or close. The purpose of the forecasts is to develop a range of expected prices for the next trading day, and then to use the range to chalk out a trading plan for specific contingencies. You can plan a variety of actions with the forecast, such as setting stops, initiating new positions, or closing old ones. You can estimate your risk and reward, and write orders to take profits, cut losses, or selectively add or reduce existing positions.

A T-Bond Spreadsheet

We will use the TREND function from Microsoft Excel to illustrate the use of forecasts. Table 2.2 shows the daily high, low, and close of the September, 1993 Treasury Bond contract from 01/27/1993 through 02/17/1993. The rows are numbered 1 to 16 starting at the top, and the columns are labeled A through G starting at the left; the label DATE occurs in the cell designated A1.

We used the built-in TREND function in Excel to calculate the 5-day forecast. Please notice that we inserted the forecast one day ahead of the calculations. Thus, the actual trading range and the forecast trading range are on the same line. We wrote the TREND function as follows to calculate the forecast high in cell E7:

forecast high in cell E7

$$= \text{TREND}(b2:b6,,\{6\},\text{TRUE}) \quad (2.4)$$

Table 2.2 A 5-day Forecast Developed with an Excel Spreadsheet

Date	High	Low	Close	← 5-Day Forecast →		
930127	104.5	104.156	104.313	HIGH	LOW	CLOSE
930128	104.969	104.344	104.5			
930129	105.094	104.438	104.719			
930201	104.938	104.375	104.938			
930202	104.719	104.375	104.469			
930203	104.813	104.406	104.781	104.966	104.478	104.813
930204	105.531	105.188	105.344	104.7	104.406	104.775
930205	105.906	105	105.875	105.244	105.016	105.178
930208	105.844	105.563	105.563	106.006	105.287	105.906
930209	105.688	105.219	105.438	106.366	105.797	106.191
930210	105.563	104.563	104.625	106.175	105.675	105.859
930211	105.5	104.563	105.344	105.659	104.797	104.806
930212	105.844	105.031	105.5	105.372	104.419	104.769
930216	106.156	105.219	105.375	105.631	104.472	105.228
930217	105.875	105.344	105.844	106.116	105.059	105.481

This defines the first five values of the high in cells B2 through B6 as the ones to be used for the forecast. By not specifying the range of x values, we are using the default values 1, 2, 3, 4, 5 for the five days. This is exactly what we did in Table 2.1 earlier. The {6} gives us the forecast for the next trading day. The last item, TRUE, says that the intercept should be calculated as usual. This ensures that the best-fit line will not go through the origin.

Note that we always use the days 1, 2, 3, 4, 5 as the independent x variables for each successive forecast. We forecast the high for day 6 using data from days 1 through 5; for day 7, we use data from days 2 through 7, dropping the data from day 1. Accordingly, we assume that the market's "memory" extends five days back. We will show how to extend the calculation to cell E8 using the TREND function:

forecast high in cell E8
$$= \text{TREND(b3:b7,,\{6\},TRUE)} \quad (2.5)$$

Forecasts for the low and the close use exactly the same calculation method. If you do not have a TREND function in your spreadsheet, you can use the calculation scheme shown in Table 2.1. For completeness, we will show how we wrote the TREND function for forecasting the low and the close. In effect, you can use the COPY function in the spreadsheet to copy the formula from cell E7 into the neighboring columns, cells F7 and G7. Similarly, you can then copy the formula from these cells into all subsequent rows to calculate the remaining forecasts.

forecast low in cell F7 = TREND(c2:c6,,{6},TRUE)
forecast close in cell G7 = TREND(d2:d6,,{6},TRUE)

$$(2.6)$$

Graphs for T-Bond Forecasts

The daily range and 5-day forecast for the September 1993 Treasury Bond contract is shown in Figure 2.12. This market was making swing moves in February and March, 1993. You

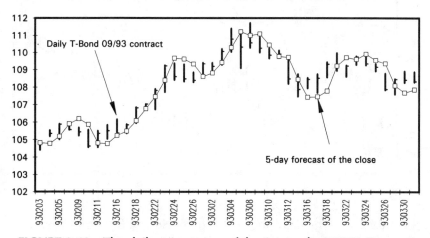

FIGURE 2.12   The daily price range of the September, 1993 Treasury Bond futures contract and a 5-day forecast of the daily close.

can see that a close above or below the forecast tipped off the trend for the next several days. For example, a close above the forecast on February 11 led into a tradeable 8-day rally. The market corrected briefly by going sideways for three days. It resumed another small four-day swing, leading to a short-term top near 111–16. The next series of swing moves were also tradeable on a short-term basis.

Figure 2.13 shows the same T-Bond 09/93 contract in the months of April, May, and June, 1993, indicating the envelopes formed by the 5-day forecast of the daily highs and lows. The envelopes tend to narrow before significant moves. A daily close outside the envelope also provided clues of future market direction. For example, note the close above the high forecast in early April, May, and June that led to higher prices. A close below the envelope also preceded down moves in mid-April and mid-May. The envelope often acted as a point of resistance and support as the market searched for direction, and could be used to plan trading strategy.

The T-Bond market trended steadily upward in June 1993. It was not making large swing moves. Figure 2.14 shows the

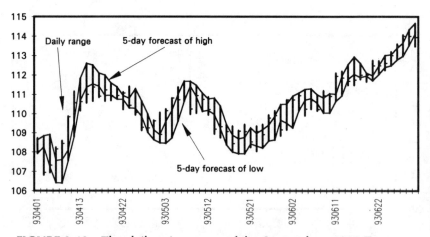

FIGURE 2.13   The daily price range of the September, 1993 Treasury Bond futures contract and a 5-day forecast envelope.

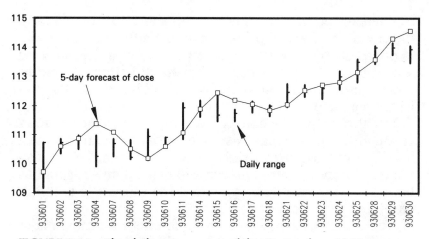

FIGURE 2.14 The daily price range of the September, 1993 Treasury Bond futures contract and a 5-day forecast of the daily close.

daily forecast close and price range. Here, too, a close above the forecast helped gauge market direction. Nevertheless, the market often traded in a narrow range in this month; therefore, not every close below the forecast led to down moves.

Contingency Planning with the Forecast "Template"

The daily forecast is usually a good guess for the next trading day, and can be used as a template. When the market is particularly strong or weak, it closes above the forecast high or below the forecast low. The most important benefit of using the forecast template is that you will have specific numbers for planning actions if the market trades at or beyond a particular price.

The types of plans you can develop are varied. One simple strategy is to buy or sell on the close. Let's assume that the close is going to be above the forecast for that day. You could then buy on the close, expecting higher prices ahead.

Another approach is to use the daily forecast high and low

as reference points. You could try to short near the highs of the day if you feel a short-term top or trading range is about to occur. Conversely, you could try to buy near the projected low of the day if you expect a short-term bottom or trading range. To trade with the trend, you could buy above the projected high and sell below the low.

You also can use the daily forecast high and low to set stops. If you are long, you may wish to cash out below the forecast low. You can use the forecast for with-the-trend or against-the-trend trades. Your approach will depend on your trading horizon and market strategy. Thus, the forecast is useful in developing a game plan for trading.

We have analyzed the regression forecasts for most major futures markets by counting the number of times the market closed above the forecast high or below the forecast low from 01/01/87 to 03/01/93. On average, the market closed beyond the forecast 66 percent of the time. For example, over 1552 trading days, the Treasury Bond market closed above the forecast high on 516 days and below the forecast low on 484 days. A close beyond the forecasts often provides a tradeable signal of short-term market strength or weakness.

DEVELOPING A FORECAST OSCILLATOR

To develop an oscillator based on the forecast, you simply subtract the forecast from the close, and express it as a percentage of the close. This forecast oscillator will be positive if the close is above the forecast. You can combine it with a simple moving average to get an early signal of a potential trend change. You also can use it as an overbought/oversold indicator.

In Table 2.3, we show the calculations using the same data for the 5-day forecast from Table 2.2. We define the forecast oscillator %F as follows:

$$\%F = 100*(C - C_f)/C \tag{2.7}$$

Table 2.3 Forecast Oscillator Calculations

Date	Close	Forecast Close	Forecast Oscillator of Close
930127	104.3125		
930128	104.5		
930129	104.7188		
930201	104.9375		
930202	104.4688		
930203	104.7813	104.81255	−1
930204	105.3438	104.77506	18
930205	105.875	105.17818	22
930208	105.5625	105.90628	−12
930209	105.4375	106.19061	−25
930210	104.625	105.85935	−40
930211	105.3438	104.80623	17
930212	105.5	104.76879	23
930216	105.375	105.22815	4
930217	105.8437	105.48126	11

Here, C is the daily close and C_f is today's forecast close from the previous five daily closes. Multiplication by 100 could be changed to multiplication by any suitable scaling constant. In the calculations above we have converted the %F into ticks of 1/32nds of a point, since that is the smallest increment in which the T-Bond contract is traded. For example, for 02/03/93, the difference between the actual close and the forecast was −0.03125. Multiplying this by 32 converts the difference into −1/32 or −1 tick. We converted the difference into an integer for convenience.

Figure 2.15 shows the forecast oscillator of the close and its 3-day simple moving average. The oscillator shows the difference between the actual close and the forecast close expressed in 1/32nds or ticks. A close below the forecast close gives negative values, predicting lower prices ahead. The crossover of the oscillator and its moving average gave early

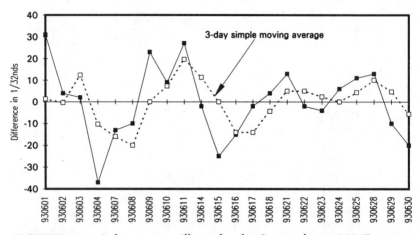

FIGURE 2.15   A forecast oscillator for the September, 1993 Treasury Bond futures contract.

warnings, which are useful for planning a trading strategy. You can see the actual market action of the September, 1993 T-Bond contract in Figure 2.14. For example, note the crossover in Figure 2.15 on 06/03/93 and 06/17/93. You can see a decisive failure on 06/14/93 as %F closed well below its trailing moving average. Despite that, the actual close was practically the same as the forecast.

In practice, you could also develop a forecast oscillator for the high and the low. This can provide more information on potential trend changes.

SUMMARY

The linear regression method provides the slope and r², the coefficient of determination. You can measure trendiness with r² since the slope can be used for following price trends. The slope can also be used to identify overbought or oversold conditions and to develop forecasts for the next trading day that can be used to develop a game plan for your trading.

Clearly, the linear regression method is a flexible analysis tool that can be easily adapted to your trading style.

Tutorial: Linear Regression Analysis

The linear regression method tries to fit an equation of the form:

$$y = m * x + C \qquad (2.8)$$

to the data. In this equation, x is the independent variable, y is the dependent variable, m is the slope of the line and C is the y-axis intercept; in effect, C is a constant. Assume that by visual inspection, we can deduce approximate values of the slope and intercept. We will call these approximate values M0 and C0. Once we know M0 and C0, we can calculate values of y_i. At each point, we will have an error term, defined as:

$$e_i = y - y_i = y - (M0 * x_i + C0) \qquad (2.9)$$

Here, the subscript ($_i$) denotes different values of the independent variable x. The least squares method minimizes the sum of the squares of the error terms. The error term is the vertical deviation from the line to the actual data at that value of x; the deviation can be positive or negative. By squaring the deviation, we get only positive numbers. The linear regression finds the particular values of slope and intercept that minimize the sum of the squared deviations. Note that the first useful piece of information from linear regression is the slope. Once we know the slope and the intercept, we can draw or calculate the best-fit line for different values of x.

We will now calculate two deviations. The first deviation is the vertical distance between the fitted line and a given data point:

$$e_f = y - y_f \qquad\qquad (2.10)$$

Here we have used the subscript $_f$ to show the error from the best-fit line. If we squared each deviation e_f and added them, we would have the SSE or Sum of Squares from fitting errors. Thus:

$$SSE = sum\ (e_f)^2 \qquad\qquad (2.11)$$

where we sum over all data points.

Next, we calculate the average of all values of y, the dependent variable. We can now measure the deviation of each value of y from y_g, the average value of all y values, or:

$$y_a = (y - y_g) \qquad\qquad (2.12)$$

We can now define SST or sum of squares total, which is the sum of all the terms in Equation 2.11. SST is the sum of squared deviations of each y from the average value of the dependent variable. We define SST as:

$$SST = sum\ (y_a)^2 \qquad\qquad (2.13)$$

We expect SSE to be less than SST, since the method of least squares minimizes the deviations from the fitted line. Intuitively, we can expect SSE to be 0 if all the points fall perfectly on a straight line. Every point that moves away from the best-fit straight line will increase SSE.

In the worst case, the fitted line is no better than a horizontal line drawn at the average value of y, and the deviations will be the same as the deviation from the average value of y. Hence, SSE will equal SST. We can now define a quantity to measure the strength of the linear relationship. This quantity is r^2, the coefficient of determination defined as:

$$r^2 = (SST - SSE) / SST \qquad (2.14)$$

In the best case, with all points on a straight line, SSE = 0, and $r^2 = 1$; ithe worst case, SSE = SST and $r^2 = 0$. The coefficient of determination is the ratio of the variation explained by the line to the total variation in y. By definition, we know that when r^2 is 0, the slope of the regression line is also 0. We can now say that r^2 is a measure of the relative strength of the linear relationship, thus of the trendiness in the data.

We can draw statistical inferences from the linear regression with a 90 or 95 percent confidence level. For example, we can test the hypothesis that the slope of the linear regression is 0. If the slope is statistically significant, we will reject the null hypothesis that the slope is 0. The usual process for testing a hypothesis is to set up an analysis of variance (ANOVA) table to calculate the F-statistic. The ANOVA table is shown in Table 2.4.

Here, n is the number of days in the linear regression. For us, the value of n was 14 days, so the error term will have 12 degrees of freedom. We have already defined SSE and SST in our calculations of r^2. With a confidence level of, say, 90 percent, we look up the value of the F-ratio with 90 percent

Table 2.4 ANOVA Table for Linear Regression

Source of Variation	Degrees of Freedom	Sum of Squares	Mean Square	F-ratio
Regression model	1	SSR	MSR=SSR/1	MSR/MSE
Error (residual)	(n − 2)	SSE	MSE = SSE/ (n − 2)	
Total	(n − 1)	SST		

n = number of days in regression

confidence level, and 1 and 12 degrees of freedom. (You can find the F-ratio tables in most introductory books on statistics.)

Note two important values of F-ratio: 3.18 and 4.75. With a 90 percent confidence level, the F-ratio must exceed 3.18 to yield a statistically significant slope. Similarly, the F-ratio must exceed 4.75 for the slope to be statistically significant with 95 percent confidence level. Both values are for a 14-day regression.

We will rewrite the F-ratio in terms of r^2 for ease of computation, and use the relationship $SST = SSE + SSR$ for simplifying the equation below. We also will use the definition of r^2.

$$
\begin{aligned}
\text{F-ratio} &= MSR/MSE \\
&= (n - 2) * (SSR/SSE) \\
&= (n - 2) * (SST - SSE)/SSE \qquad\qquad (2.15) \\
&= (n - 2) * r_2 * (1/(SSE/SST)) \\
&= (n - 2) * (r^2/(1 - r^2))
\end{aligned}
$$

This equation says that, as r^2 increases, the F-ratio increases, and we are more likely to have a significant slope. Remember, the important values of F-ratio are 3.18 and 4.75 for a 14-day linear regression. We can substitute these values into the F-ratio equation and find the critical values of r^2 that yield statistically significant slopes. We can therefore express r^2 in terms of the F-ratio:

$$
\begin{aligned}
G &= F/(n-2) \qquad\qquad\qquad\qquad\qquad (2.16) \\
r^2 &= G/(1+G)
\end{aligned}
$$

Here, F is the F-ratio for a given confidence level, with 1 and $(n - 2)$ degrees of freedom. From the equation for G, the critical values are 0.21 and 0.29 (rounded). These correspond to a confidence level of 90 and 95 percent (see Table 2.5). Thus, when the r^2 value exceeds 0.29, the slope is statistically significant.

You can find values of the F-ratio from an introductory book on statistics to calculate the critical values for any regression you wish. We tabulated at length the critical values for linear regressions of 10 to 50 days in length in Table 2.6. The confidence level was 95 percent for all calculations in that table. The slope is statistically significant when the coefficient of determination of the regression is greater than the critical value.

Table 2.6 shows that as the number of days in the linear regression increases, the critical value of r^2 decreases. Thus, it is easier to spot trends as the length of the regression increases. When the calculated value of r^2 is less than its critical value, then the slope is not statistically different from 0. We

Table 2.5 Critical Values of r^2

Confidence Level	Critical Value of r^2
90 percent with 1 and 12 DOF	0.2095 (0.21 rounded)
95 percent with 1 and 12 DOF	0.2836 (0.29 rounded)

Slope of 14-day regression is statistically significant if critical value of r^2 is exceeded.

Table 2.6 Critical Values of r^2

n (days)	DOF = n − 2	F-ratio 0.95,1,n − 2	G = F/ (n − 2)	r^2 Critical = G/(1 + G)
10	8	5.32	0.665	0.40
20	18	4.41	0.245	0.20
30	28	4.20	0.150	0.13
50	48	4.04	0.084	0.08

Slope of n day regression is statistically significant if critical value is exceeded. Confidence level = 95 percent.

n = Number of days in the regression
DOF = Degrees of freedom
Values of r^2 are rounded.

can then say that the data have no statistically significant trend.

You will find that high values of r^2 often occur with high values of slope. The value of r^2 is close to 0 when the slope is changing signs. Consequently, you should consider both the slope and r^2 in your analysis.

3
The Variable Index
Dynamic Average

Change is the only constant in life, and nowhere is it more evident than on the trading floor. Our financial and futures markets seem to change every minute of every day. These markets are dynamic because traders constantly adjust to changing perceptions and participants. Yet, in spite of this dynamism, we usually use static indicators in our analysis, and these static indicators don't change the time period of analysis. For example, many traders use a 9-day or 14-day period to calculate their technical indicators such as RSI, the relative strength index.

Dynamic indicators, in contrast, vary the time period used in analyzing market action. In this chapter we will show you how to use the variable index dynamic average (VIDYA), a dynamic exponential moving average that adjusts its effective length using a market variable. For instance, we will index VIDYA to the standard deviation of closing prices, as well as to a momentum oscillator, and to the coefficient of determination, r^2. The responsiveness and dynamic range of VIDYA changes with the indexing approach, and you can adapt it to suit your needs.

THE SIMPLE MOVING AVERAGE
AND ITS RESPONSIVENESS

A simple moving average (SMA) uses a fixed number of days to calculate a new value. For instance, when we use the most recent 10 days' data to calculate a 10-day simple moving average, we disregard market volatility. Unfortunately, the gap between the current price and the moving average usually increases when the market moves quickly. In percentage terms, the price gap could easily be 1–20 percent from the moving average.

Let's consider two simple moving averages of the daily closing price; let the shorter moving average use five days and the longer average use ten days. If the market makes a quick move, the shorter moving average will respond earlier than the longer moving average. In the 5-day SMA calculations, each of the daily closes, including the latest close, has a weight of 20 percent. The 10-day SMA assigns a weight of 10 percent to the latest daily close. The shorter average responds more quickly than the longer one because it uses a greater proportion of new data, and usually has a smaller price gap between the latest price and the moving average.

These calculations are simulated in Table 3.1. The columns show how the 20 percent slice of new data makes the 5-day SMA more responsive to price changes than the 10-day SMA. For example, in the last row, the close is 14.75 percent above the 5-day SMA. The same close is 20.48 percent above the 10-day SMA. Thus, the more responsive average has narrowed the gap between itself and the latest close.

This table illustrates the key idea behind a variable length moving average: We can make the average responsive to data by reducing its length when volatility increases, or increasing it when volatility decreases. By making these changes automatically, if possible, the average could adapt its length to market action.

Table 3.1 Comparing Responsiveness of 5-Day and 10-Day SMAs

Close	20% of Close	10% of Close	5-day SMA	10-day SMA
100	20.00	10.00		
125	25.00	12.50		
110	22.00	11.00		
90	18.00	9.00		
108	21.60	10.80	106.60	
119	23.80	11.90	110.40	
135	27.00	13.50	112.40	
110	22.00	11.00	112.40	
100	20.00	10.00	114.40	
125	25.00	12.50	117.80	112.20
140	28.00	14.00	122.00	116.20

The 5-day SMA gives an equal weight of 20 percent to 5 day's data.
The 10-day SMA gives an equal weight of 10 percent to 10 day's data.
The 5-day SMA responds faster because it takes a larger bite out of new data.

A Volatility Index

We need a volatility index to tell us when the price action is heating up or cooling down. Volatility can be measured as the standard deviation in the closing prices over the past x days.

In order to form the index, we also need a reference value of the standard deviation over x days. The reference value will tell us if the observed standard deviation is too high or too low. Then, we can define a volatility index that refers current volatility to historical volatility as:

$$k = \text{sigma(x-days) / sigma(reference)}. \qquad (3.1)$$

Here, sigma(x-days) is the standard deviation of closing prices over x days. sigma(reference) is the historical value of the standard deviation over x days. For example, you could use a 20-day moving average of sigma as the reference value.

This would then become the historical reference value of sigma. You also could use the average value of sigma over a time period of 5 times that used to calculate the standard deviation.

A third approach is to find the maximum and minimum value of the standard deviation over x days. You can then choose an arbitrary value for the reference that is 1/4 or 1/5 the maximum value.

Our next problem is to choose a moving average. We will work with an exponential moving average. The mathematics of exponential averages requires that its index be a constant. However, we will arbitrarily deviate from this logic by making the index a variable. You can visualize this as calculating a new exponential average each day. Rather than using a fixed fraction to update the new value, we will use a changing fraction. Our series of numbers will then represent values of exponential moving averages with variable length.

We can now write an equation for VIDYA using the usual equation for exponential moving averages:

$$\text{VIDYA} = \text{alpha} * k * C_0 + (1 - \text{alpha} * k) * C_1. \qquad (3.2)$$

In this equation, today's close and yesterday's close have the subscripts 0 and 1; we have previously defined the volatility index, k. The constant, alpha, determines the effective length of the exponential moving average we want to modulate. When $k = 1$, we have an exponential average determined by alpha. When $k > 1$, we take a larger bite of the new data and the effective length of the average decreases. When $k < 1$, we take a smaller bite out of the new data, and the effective length of the average then increases. In choosing values for alpha and k, we must ensure that the term $(1 - \text{alpha} * k)$ never becomes negative.

Dynamic Range of VIDYA

We can now estimate the equivalent length of an exponential moving average from the index. For example, let N be the number of days in an exponential moving average. The index, alpha, of the average is given in the following equation:

$$alpha = (2/(N + 1)). \hspace{3cm} (3.3)$$

We can solve for N in terms of alpha:

$$N = (2 - alpha)/alpha.$$

We can insert a known value of alpha to solve for the number of days in the moving average. We will do just that, by building a table to show how the length of VIDYA changes as the volatility index changes (Table 3.2).

This table shows that, as the market enters a quiet phase and k < 1, the length of VIDYA increases. Conversely, when the market is active and k > 1, the length of VIDYA decreases. VIDYA will simulate a 9-day exponential moving average when the product of k and alpha is 0.20. As the product of

Table 3.2 Dynamic Range and Effective Length of VIDYA

Volatility (Index, k)	Alpha (Index for 9-day EMA)	k*Alpha (Index for VIDYA)	No. Days in Average (effective length)
0.20	0.20	0.04	49.00
0.40	0.20	0.08	24.00
0.60	0.20	0.12	15.67
0.80	0.20	0.16	11.50
1.00	0.20	0.20	9.00
1.20	0.20	0.24	7.33
1.40	0.20	0.28	6.14
1.60	0.20	0.32	5.25
1.80	0.20	0.36	4.56
2.00	0.20	0.40	4.00

A 9-day exponential moving average (EMA) has alpha = 0.20.
The effective length of a VIDYA = (2 − k* alpha)/(k * alpha).
The dynamic range is the range of effective lengths = 49 − 4 = 45.

k * alpha varies tenfold from 0.04 to 0.4 due to rising volatility, the effective length of VIDYA decreases from 49 to 4
days, a wide dynamic range. An exponential moving average
with a length of 49 days is much slower than one with a length
of 4 days. Therefore, VIDYA will move faster than the equivalent exponential moving average in response to rising market
volatility.

TRADING STRATEGIES

All your usual strategies with moving averages can be used
with VIDYA. For example, you can use a short and a long
VIDYA and use a moving average crossover decision model.
Or, you can take the difference between the two averages and
trade that with a third moving average, which is the MACD
or moving average convergence-divergence approach discussed in Chapters 1 and 2. You can use moving averages
and trading bands or use VIDYA to set trailing stops. Since
VIDYA adjusts its length automatically in response to market
volatility, it will generally remain closer to prices than the
equivalent exponential moving average. Hence, its responsiveness can give you more timely trades, which is the main
advantage of using VIDYA.

You can use volatility bands around VIDYA to make trading decisions and create a breakout system, trading prices in
the direction of their breakout outside the bands. Your next
signal to close the trade or reverse is when prices close inside
the bands for the first time. You also can use bands shifted
above and below VIDYA by a fixed percentage, such as 1
percent. The upper and lower bands act as points of support
and resistance. When prices close near the upper or lower
band, you would look for market reversals. As usual, when
the market is trending strongly, it can close outside the bands.
This is a signal that the trend will persist. You would then
wait for the prices to close inside the bands before taking
countertrend positions.

CASE IN POINT: VIDYA AND T-BOND MARKET ANALYSIS

Figure 3.1 shows the US Bond 06/93 contract along with VIDYA and an equivalent exponential moving average. You can easily see that VIDYA is more responsive than the exponential moving average. The effective length of VIDYA is shown in Figure 3.2 for the data in Figure 3.1. The units of the y-axis are the number of days in the equivalent exponential moving average. You will see that, as volatility increases, the effective length of VIDYA decreases. For example, observe the decrease in length in February, 1993 as the market moved up quickly. You can see that VIDYA automatically adjusts its length to daily changes in market volatility. Notice how VIDYA moved up during 02/93 in Figure 3.1.

You also can use VIDYA to set unique trailing stops on a closing basis. For example, if you were long, you would close your long tomorrow if the market closed below VIDYA today and was going to close lower tomorrow. Or, you can go long when prices close above VIDYA, and go short when prices close below VIDYA. As an aggressive trader you could anticipate a close above or below VIDYA to initiate your trade. This would let you put on a position a day earlier than discussed above. VIDYA lets you set unique stops that cannot be gunned easily.

Shifted Trading Bands

Figure 3.3 shows an example of VIDYA and 1 percent trading bands. You could experiment with bands of different separations if you wish. The lower band, drawn 1 percent below VIDYA, acted as support for closing prices during the correction from record highs in March. Notice that the initial low on 03/26/93 at the band led to the lower low also at the lower band. You could have gone long the T-Bond when it

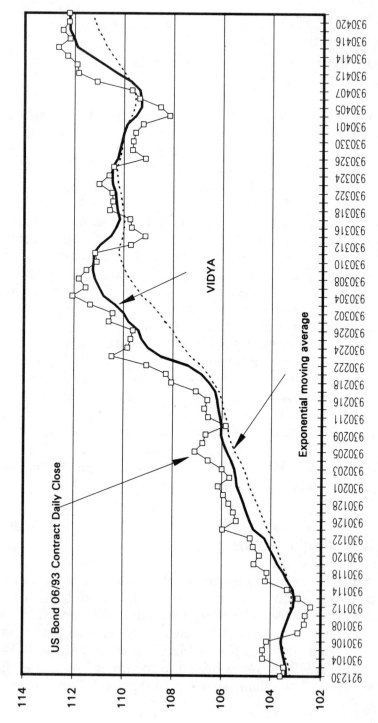

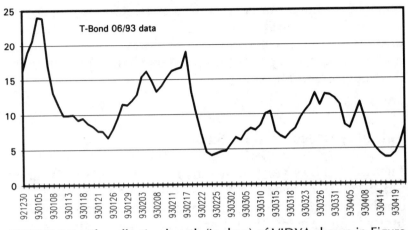

FIGURE 3.2   The effective length (in days) of VIDYA shown in Figure 3.1.

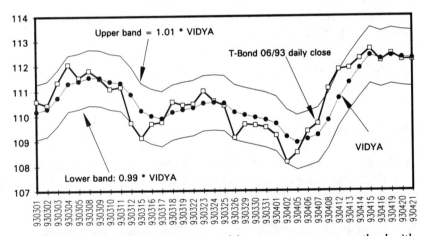

FIGURE 3.3   The June, 1993, T-Bond futures contract, smoothed with a variable index dynamic average.

bounced off the lower band, with a close stop for proper risk control. During the upward move in April, 1993, prices closed outside the upper 1 percent band, showing a strong upward move. As expected, prices continued their climb for four more days before moving sideways.

Volatility-Based Trading Bands

Figure 3.4 shows volatility bands formed using the dynamic range values derived for VIDYA calculations. These bands can be traded as a breakout system, since a close above the upper band or below the lower band often presents tradeable opportunities. Details of the calculations are in the tutorial at the end of the chapter.

Another use of the bands is to define trendiness. The market is trending up if the close is outside the upper band; conversely, the market is trending down if the close is below the lower band. You also could use the direction of the bands to judge the trend. A close within the bands predicts a trendless or consolidation phase.

Indexing to Momentum or r^2

Another useful feature of VIDYA is that it can be indexed to any dimensionless market variable that varies from 0 to 1. Thus, you don't need the standard deviation to calculate VIDYA. For example, you could index VIDYA to the coefficient of determination, r^2, since r^2 measures trendiness, is dimensionless, and varies between 0 and 1. You could also index VIDYA to a momentum oscillator that varies between 0 and 1, such as the relative strength index (RSI). We like using the absolute value of the 9-day Chande momentum oscillator (CMO) as the momentum index. The CMO, a variant of the RSI, is described in Chapter 5.

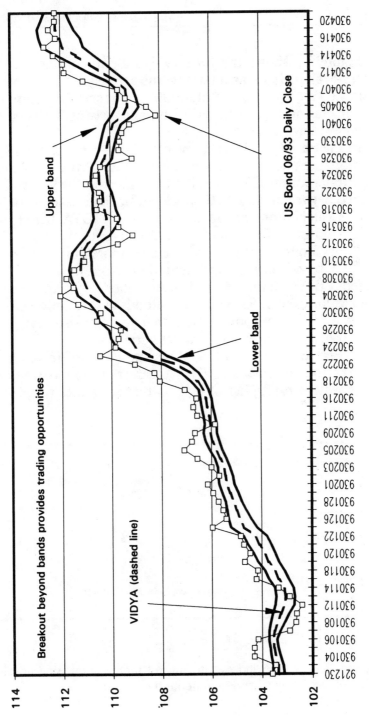

Breakout beyond bands provides trading opportunities

Upper band

VIDYA (dashed line)

Lower band

US Bond 06/93 Daily Close

59

Figure 3.5 shows the June 1993 T-Bond contract in February-March, 1993, as it became the actively traded contract. The VIDYA, based on absolute CMO, was sensitive to market action during rapid moves. Simultaneously, it flattened out during sideways periods.

In Figure 3.6, one VIDYA is calculated using standard deviation and another uses a 9-day absolute CMO. The scaling multiplier for the CMO was 0.50. This means the 9-day CMO varied between 0 and 0.50 for these calculations. (The details of the calculations are in the tutorial.) VIDYA based on a scaled, absolute CMO was more sensitive for the June, 1993 Treasury Bond contract. It accelerated more quickly than the VIDYA based on standard deviation. Note how the CMO-based VIDYA flattened out in December, 1992 and accelerated in January, 1993. The two methods of calculation change the way VIDYA responds. Note that you can also change the sensitivity by altering the scaling variables.

In Figure 3.7, we look at the same contract in the same time period, but calculate VIDYA using r^2. Here too, we scaled the r^2 with a multiplier of 0.50 so that its values range from

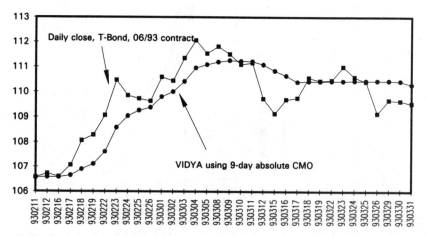

FIGURE 3.5 VIDYA indexed to market momentum using absolute value of the 9-day Chande momentum oscillator.

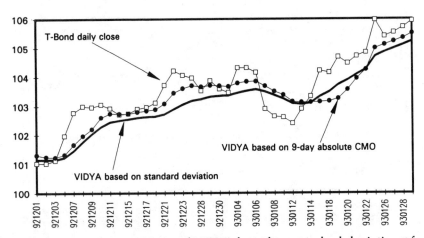

FIGURE 3.6 A comparison of VIDYA based on standard deviation of closing prices and the 9-day absolute Chande momentum oscillator.

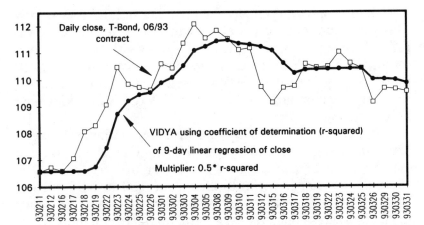

FIGURE 3.7 A variable index dynamic average that was indexed to market action using 0.5 times the coefficient of determination (r^2) from a 9-day linear regression analysis of the daily close.

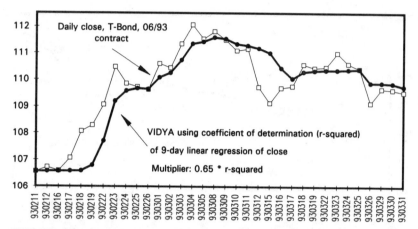

FIGURE 3.8 A VIDYA for the June 1993 T-Bond daily close similar to the one in Figure 3.7. We used 0.65 times the r² value from the 9-day linear regression to calculate VIDYA.

0 to 0.50. You can compare Figures 3.6 and 3.7 to see how changing the indexing variable changed the response of VI-DYA. When the linear regression analysis showed a strong trend, the VIDYA based on r² accelerated rapidly. It moved more quickly than the VIDYA based on the absolute CMO; for example, compare the two types of VIDYA in mid-to-late February.

Not only can you change the indexing variable, but you can also change the scaling variable. In Figure 3.8 you can see the effect of using a new multiplier of 0.65 for r². The effect of the change in multiplier from 0.50 to 0.65 did not make much difference when the market was trendless. Once the linear regression detected a trend on 02/19/93, the VIDYA with the higher multiplier moved more quickly. Notice how the VIDYA flattened out as r² decreased during consolidations. You can use a VIDYA based on r² to set aggressive trailing stops that are unique and not easily gunned.

SUMMARY

These examples show what occurred when we used three different approaches to calculate VIDYA: a volatility index based on the standard deviation of closing prices, a momentum oscillator, and the strength of the linear trend (r^2) from linear regression analysis. VIDYA automatically adapted to market action and selected an effective length based on the indexing method. We also saw that the scaling multiplier for each method can be changed to increase the dynamic range of VIDYA and make it more sensitive to price changes.

Not only can you trade with VIDYA using the usual moving average trading strategies, but you can also use it to set unique trailing stops or develop volatility bands for a breakout trading system. Finally, you can use shifted bands to find resistance and support. In short, VIDYA is a highly flexible moving average that you can easily adapt to suit your trading style.

TUTORIAL: SPREADSHEETS FOR VIDYA

Once you go through the steps of setting up VIDYA, you can use it for many of your own strategies. Since it is a moving average, all the usual moving average strategies can be applied. For example, you could use the crossover of two moving averages to generate trading signals, or you could use the moving average to set trailing stops.

Calculating VIDYA Using Standard Deviation

First, we want to use a market volatility index to assess price action. To illustrate, we will use data for the Treasury Bond March, 1993 contract with the 10-day standard deviation of closing prices to define volatility. The 50-day average of the 10-day standard deviation was 0.64. The range of values for the 10-day standard deviation was from a low of 0.13 to a high of 1.47. Here is the range of values of the volatility index (with rounding):

$$k = 0.13/0.64 = 0.21 \qquad\qquad (3.4)$$
$$k = 1.47/0.64 = 2.29$$

Note that we calculated the volatility index k by using a reference value of 0.64. We obtained the reference value by averaging 50 days of data on the 10-day standard deviation. You could also have chosen an arbitrary reference value. For example, the range of values for the 10-day standard deviation of the close was 0.13 to 1.47. If you had arbitrarily chosen a reference value of 1, the range of k would be from 0.13 to 2.29. The key is to ensure that the term $(1-k*alpha)$ always remains positive. Hence, if you were using a value of 0.1 for alpha, then the quantity $(1-k*alpha)$ would be positive for a reference value of 1. You can test a range of values to choose a responsiveness of VIDYA you like.

We will use a 19-day exponential moving average, with an alpha of 0.1, given by the ratio of $2/(19+1)$ or 2/20. The dynamism of this VIDYA can be calculated from the range of values in Table 3.3. Thus, we will effectively vary the number of days in the exponential average all the way from about 8 to about 94. The equivalent exponential moving average would always use 19 days.

Table 3.4 illustrates the start of calculations in a spreadsheet format. We first calculated the 10-day standard deviation of the close (0.96), and then divided it by 0.64 to find the k value

Table 3.3 The Dynamism of Vidya

k	Alpha	k * Alpha	No. of Days (rounded)
0.21	0.1	.021	94
1	0.1	0.1	19
2.29	0.1	0.229	8

Table 3.4 VIDYA Calculations

Date	Close	10-day StdDev	k=c/0.64	VIDYA	EXPMA
921127	102.00				
921130	101.97				
921201	102.19				
921202	102.19				
921203	102.31				
921204	103.16				
921207	103.97				
921208	104.19				
921209	104.19			104.19	104.19
921210	104.25	0.96	1.50	104.20	104.19
921211	104.13	0.94	1.47	104.19	104.19
921214	103.88	0.85	1.33	104.15	104.16
921215	103.91	0.74	1.16	104.12	104.13
921216	104.09	0.58	0.91	104.12	104.13
921217	104.13	0.30	0.47	104.12	104.13

of 1.50. We used the previous day's (92/12/09) close to find the first value of VIDYA. The first value for 92/12/10 is 104.20, calculated by using

$$VIDYA = (0.1*1.5)*104.25 + (1-0.1*1.5)*104.19$$
$$= 104.20. \tag{3.5}$$

The corresponding exponential averaged has an alpha of 0.1. It is shown in the last column. We continue the calculations for all later days. At the end of February, 1993, there was a sharp rally in the bond market in reaction to President Clinton's budget proposals. The volatility increased and VIDYA responded more quickly than the equivalent exponential moving average. Table 3.5 shows these calculations.

As the volatility increased from 93/02/22 to 93/02/26, the values of k increased rapidly too. This increase made VIDYA take a larger chunk out of the new data. However, the equiv-

Table 3.5 VIDYA Calculations

Date	Close	10-day StdDev	c/0.64 'k'	VIDYA	EXPMA
930201	107.41	0.59	0.93	106.15	106.02
930202	106.94	0.55	0.86	106.22	106.11
930203	107.25	0.46	0.72	106.29	106.23
930204	107.81	0.44	0.69	106.40	106.38
930205	108.34	0.48	0.75	106.54	106.58
930208	108.03	0.53	0.83	106.67	106.73
930209	107.91	0.50	0.79	106.76	106.84
930210	107.09	0.47	0.73	106.79	106.87
930211	107.81	0.44	0.69	106.86	106.96
930212	107.97	0.43	0.68	106.93	107.06
930216	107.84	0.43	0.67	107.00	107.14
930217	108.31	0.38	0.59	107.07	107.26
930218	109.34	0.54	0.85	107.27	107.47
930219	109.56	0.70	1.09	107.52	107.68
930222	110.31	0.94	1.47	107.93	107.94
930223	111.72	1.35	2.11	108.73	108.32
930224	111.09	1.47	2.30	109.27	108.60
930225	110.97	1.40	2.19	109.64	108.83
930226	110.88	1.33	2.08	109.90	109.04

alent exponential moving average continued to use 19 days
in its calculations.

You also can see the responsiveness in this table. From 93/
02/19 to 93/92/24, VIDYA increased by 1.75, when the exponential moving average increased by just 0.92. VIDYA
went from 107.52 to 109.27, while the exponential moving
average went from 107.68 to 108.60. These calculations show
that VIDYA follows prices more closely than the equivalent
exponential moving average, a feature traders can exploit to
their advantage using a broad variety of strategies.

Calculating Volatility Bands with VIDYA

To develop volatility bands using VIDYA (see Table 3.6), we calculate the VIDYA as shown above, and then add the volatility-based components to form the bands. We first calculate the 10-day standard deviation in closing price. We then find the index k by dividing the standard deviation value by 0.64. This gives us the volatility-based term. Next, we must multiply these terms by the index value of the equivalent exponential moving average. We can then add any amount of this term to VIDYA to form the upper band.

Using a multiplier of 2, we add and subtract 2 times the volatility term from VIDYA. For example, for 92/12/10, we

Table 3.6   VIDYA Volatility Band Calculations

Date	Close	10-day StdDev	StdDev/ 0.64 = 'k'	VIDYA	Upper Band VIDYA + 2*.1*k k	Lower Band VIDYA − 2*.1*k
921127	102.00					
921130	101.97					
921201	102.19					
921202	102.19					
921203	102.31					
921204	103.16					
921207	103.97					
921208	104.19					
921209	104.19			104.19		
921210	104.25	0.96	1.50	104.20	104.50	103.90
921211	104.13	0.94	1.47	104.19	104.48	103.89
921214	103.88	0.85	1.33	104.15	104.41	103.88
921215	103.91	0.74	1.16	104.12	104.35	103.88
921216	104.09	0.58	0.91	104.12	104.30	103.93
921217	104.13	0.30	0.47	104.12	104.21	104.02
921218	104.28	0.13	0.21	104.12	104.16	104.08
921221	104.88	0.26	0.41	104.15	104.23	104.07

do the following calculations, noting that 0.1 is the index of the equivalent exponential moving average:

$$
\begin{aligned}
\text{upper band} &= \text{VIDYA} + 2 * 0.1 * k \\
&= 104.20 + 2*0.1*1.50 = 104.50, \qquad (3.6) \\
\text{lower band} &= \text{VIDYA} - 2 * 0.1 * k \\
&= 104.20 - 2 * 0.1 * 1.50 = 103.90.
\end{aligned}
$$

The resultant volatility bands can be used as a breakout system. A close above the upper band is a buy signal for tomorrow, and a close today below the lower band is a sell signal for tomorrow. Once you are long, a close below the upper band is a signal to close the trade. You should be prepared to go long if prices close above the upper band again. A close inside the lower band is a signal to close open short trades.

You could develop other trading strategies using bands, such as antitrend trades. You could use VIDYA to set stops on a closing basis, or you could use a price crossover to buy or sell. This tutorial should give you a feel for the power and flexibility of using VIDYA in your trading strategy.

Calculating VIDYA Using CMO

We can use any market-related index that varies from 0 to 1 to calculate VIDYA; for example, we can use the Chande momentum oscillator (CMO) to index VIDYA.

We'll use the daily closing data for the June, 1993 Treasury Bond futures contract. Here, Mtm Up is the momentum when today's close is above yesterday's close. If today's close is below yesterday's close, Mtm Up is 0. The Mtm Dn is positive if today's close is below yesterday's close, otherwise it is 0.

In the following equation, we first define the 9-day sum of the up day (S_u) and down day momentum (S_d) as:

$$CMO = (S_u - S_d)/(S_u + S_d), \tag{3.7}$$
$$absCMO = |CMO|.$$

The CMO is the net momentum as a fraction of the absolute momentum over nine days, and it can be positive or negative. The absCMO is the absolute CMO, that is, the value of CMO without regard to its sign. CMO varies between -1 and $+1$, while absCMO varies between 0 and 1. We can now define VIDYA using absCMO.

Here we have used a scaling multiplier of 0.5 to scale absCMO, but you can experiment with other values if you wish. The benefit of using a simple scaling multiplier is that we get a linear conversion from absCMO to VIDYA. If you squared the CMO to eliminate the negative sign, then the conversion becomes nonlinear. The higher the multiplier, the more responsive the average will be. Hence:

$$VIDYA = (0.5 * absCMO)*C_0 \tag{3.8a}$$
$$+ (1-0.5 * absCMO) * VIDYA_1$$

where today's close is C_0 and $VIDYA_1$ is yesterday's value of VIDYA. Here we demonstrate our calculations by using data for 02/12/93 shown in Table 3.7:

$$S_u = 0.3125+0.5625+0.5313+0.7188+0.1563$$
$$= 2.2814,$$
$$S_d = 0.4688+0.3125+0.125+0.8126 = 1.7189,$$
$$(S_u - S_d) = 0.5625,$$
$$(S_u + S_d) = 4.0003,$$
$$CMO = 0.5625/4.003 = 0.140614, \tag{3.8b}$$
$$absCMO = 0.140614,$$
$$VIDYA_1 = 106.5625,$$
$$k = 0.5*0.140614 = 0.070307,$$
$$VIDYA = 0.070307*106.7188 + (1-0.070307)*106.5625,$$
$$VIDYA = 106.573489 = 106.5735.$$

Table 3.7 Calculating VIDYA with CMO

Date	Close	Mtm Up	Mtm Dn	9-day Abs CMO	VIDYA
930201	106.1563				
930202	105.6875	0	0.4688		
930203	106	0.3125	0		
930204	106.5625	0.5625	0		
930205	107.0938	0.5313	0		
930208	106.7813	0	0.3125		
930209	106.6563	0	0.125		
930210	105.8437	0	0.8126		
930211	106.5625	0.7188	0		106.5625
930212	106.7188	0.1563	0	0.140614	106.5735
930216	106.5938	0	0.125	0.24786	106.576
930217	107.0625	0.4687	0	0.278674	106.6438
930218	108.0625	1	0	0.352925	106.8941
930219	108.2812	0.2187	0	0.301554	107.1033
930222	109.0625	0.7813	0	0.517702	107.6104
930223	110.4688	1.4063	0	0.670306	108.5684
930224	109.8437	0	0.6251	0.727246	109.0321
930225	109.7188	0	0.1249	0.643316	109.253
930226	109.625	0	0.0938	0.599983	109.3646

Calculating VIDYA with r^2

We have seen how the coefficient of determination, r^2, is a measure of trendiness that you can calculate from linear regression analysis. Since r^2 varies between 0 and 1 and is always positive, it is a natural candidate for an indexing variable for VIDYA.

We'll use the Excel 3.0 spreadsheet for calculations, which features a built-in function, LINEST, that we can use along with the built-in function, INDEX, to calculate r^2. For more details on r^2, it's best to review the section on linear regression analysis. We'll use nine days for the length of the regression calculations.

Here, we calculated the r^2 using the INDEX and LINEST functions in Excel 3.0.

$$r^2 = \text{INDEX(LINEST(b3:b11,\$c\$2:\$c\$10,TRUE,TRUE),3)}$$
$$(3.9a)$$

We scaled this value by 0.65 or 0.50, and used it to calculate VIDYA.

Next, let's review calculations for 02/12/93 below, using data from Table 3.8:

$$
\begin{aligned}
k1 &= 0.65 * 0.1292494 = 0.08401211, \\
\text{VIDYA} &= 0.08401211 * 106.7188 \\
&+ (1-0.08401211)*106.5625, \\
&= 106.5756.
\end{aligned}
$$
$$(3.9b)$$

Table 3.8 Calculating VIDYA with r^2

Date	Close	R-Squared	VIDYA 0.65	VIDYA 0.50
930201	106.1563	1		
930202	105.6875	2		
930203	106.0	3		
930204	106.5625	4		
930205	107.0938	5		
930208	106.7813	5		
930209	106.6563	7		
930210	105.8437	8		
930211	106.5625	9	106.5625	106.5625
930212	106.7188	0.1292494	106.5756	106.5726
930216	106.5938	0.0336062	106.576	106.573
930217	107.0625	0.0022159	106.5767	106.5735
930218	108.0625	0.1889946	106.7593	106.7142

These calculations show that you can adapt VIDYA to market action using a dimensionless market-related index such as volatility, momentum oscillators, or r^2. You can adjust the scaling to increase or decrease the sensitivity of this adaptive moving average.

4

QSTICK: The Quantitative Candlestick

Originating in Japan, the candlestick method of price analysis is mainly a pattern-recognition technique. Hence, it has predictive power, unlike moving averages or oscillators. The drawback to using this approach is that pattern interpretation is very subjective, and so this method remains qualitative in nature.

Building on the basics of candlestick analysis, our new indicator, Qstick, enables you to quantify candlestick analysis and improve the interpretation of candlestick patterns. Qstick is a moving average of the difference between the daily close and the open—a difference that is at the heart of candlestick analysis.

THE BASICS OF CANDLESTICK ANALYSIS

We can draw a candlestick using the same price data found on a bar chart. Thus, a candlestick uses the open, high, low and closing prices for the time duration under study. This lets you combine candlesticks with trend lines, moving averages, trading bands and so forth.

In candlestick analysis, each day's price action appears like a candle. The body of the candle is drawn as a rectangular range between the open and close, and it is black (or filled) if the close is below the open. If the close is above the open, then the body is white (or empty). "Down days are dark" is an easy way to remember this scheme. Thin lines joining the high and low are called the upper and lower shadows, or tails.

Figure 4.1 shows a bar chart and the equivalent candlestick chart. The data are for the July, 1993 Cotton #2 futures contract. While the two charts use the same data, the candlestick chart is more striking in revealing bullish and bearish days.

Most analysts look at two important factors in evaluating candlesticks. The first element is the appearance of the new

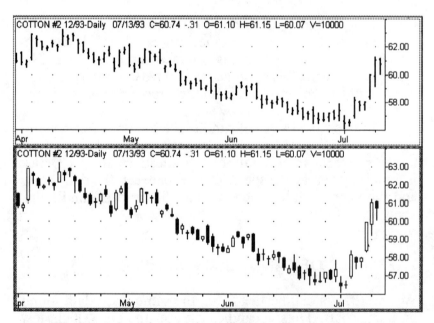

FIGURE 4.1 A bar chart and candlestick chart for the Cotton #2 futures contract using the same information for each day.

candlestick by itself. You can look at the range between the open and the close and its proportion to the shadows. But, it is the "big picture" formed using many candlesticks that is more important than a single candlestick. Often, a single candlestick is more significant when we view it within the broad technical picture.

This leads to the second and more important facet of candlestick pattern evaluation: the pattern formed by two or more candlesticks. The range between the open and the close shows the power of bulls or bears. A market has great power or conviction when the open and close are far apart. Conversely, a market lacks power or conviction when the open and close are not far apart. The length of the shadows is also important. Powerful markets have short shadows, whereas markets that are weakening or changing often show long shadows. Successive candlesticks form patterns that may suggest a strengthening or weakening of the market.

QSTICK: INTRADAY MOMENTUM INDICATOR

We have noted that the range between the open and the close is the most important element of candlestick analysis. The difference, close minus open, is a measure of intraday (or intraperiod) momentum. We have quantified this range to develop a trend-following indicator. This indicator, called Qstick, can be defined as the moving average of the intraday momentum.

We will use eight days of data for calculating the simple moving average. You can experiment with other time periods, from minutes to months.

$$\begin{aligned} \text{Qstick} &= \text{Average}((C-O),8) \quad \text{(SuperCharts formula)} \\ &= \text{Mov}((C-O),8,S) \quad \text{(Metastock formula)} \end{aligned} \quad (4.1)$$

In this equation, O is the opening price and C is the closing price. The daily range between the open and the close can be positive or negative. Qstick will be positive when the market closes above its opening price.

Note that there is some variability in the reported data on opening and closing prices. For example, the opening price could be the price of the first trade, or it could be the first trade reported, which may not be first trade executed in the pits. Or we could use the average price of all trades in the first minute of trading. The same is true for closing prices.

In our examples we will calculate Qstick with a simple moving average. (You can use an exponential moving average if you prefer.) For example, for short-term analysis of a futures market, we prefer a 5-day Qstick. If you are using weekly charts, you can use a 30-week Qstick for the long-term trend; or you can use a 5-week Qstick for intermediate-term analysis. On a daily chart, a 20-day Qstick could be used for intermediate term analysis.

Qstick Trading Strategies

You can plot Qstick over a candlestick chart to spot divergences. There is often a divergence between Qstick and the prices before significant tops and bottoms. A divergence lasting several days is the signal of an imminent trend change because of a change in intraday momentum. This occurs because intraday momentum often changes before interday momentum.

We can smooth Qstick itself with another moving average and check to see if Qstick is above or below it. When markets make giant price moves, a slackening of the momentum can be seen when Qstick crosses below (or above) its trailing average.

You can also use the Qstick idea with a combination of moving averages to generate signals. When using a short and a long moving average of the intraday momentum, a buy signal occurs when the shorter average crosses above the longer one. Hence, we interpret an increase in intraday momentum as a signal of higher prices, and a decrease in intraday momentum as a signal of lower prices. A sell signal occurs when the shorter average crosses below the longer one.

A longer-term, trend-following approach with Qstick is to use the zero crossing of the Qstick values. You will observe that a change in sign often accompanies a change in market trend. When Qstick is negative and then becomes positive, you can go long the next day. When Qstick is positive and becomes negative, you can go short the next day or close out your long position. Aggressive traders could anticipate the zero crossover and put the trade on a day earlier.

CASE IN POINT: QSTICK AND CRASH OF 1987

Figure 4.2 shows Qstick data for the Standard & Poor's-500 Index during the three months prior to the crash of 1987. We

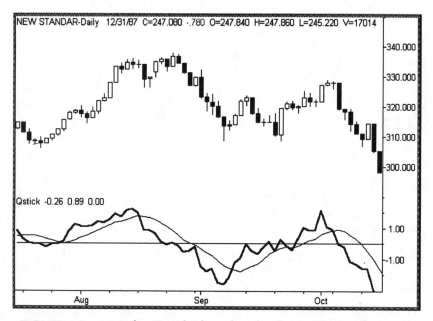

FIGURE 4.2   An 8-day Qstick plotted under the S&P-500 index in the period prior to the October, 1987 crash.

calculated Qstick with an 8-day period and also have shown an 8-day simple moving average of Qstick values. We found divergences between the index and the Qstick indicator at the August top. These divergences also occurred at the next lower high in early October. When the Qstick crossed under its moving average, a downward price move followed.

Although the Qstick analysis could not have foreseen the magnitude of the crash, it did signal a downtrend when it closed below its moving average. This happened at the 320 level on the index. Note how the Qstick was accelerating away from its own moving average leading into the crash.

This analysis does not depend on using eight days of data to calculate Qstick. You could vary the number of days and get the same results. In Figure 4.3 we show the same data as in Figure 4.2, but with a 16-day Qstick. The length of the

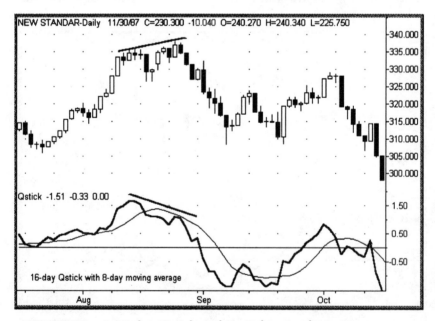

FIGURE 4.3 A 16-day Qstick and its 8-day simple moving average, shown with the Standard & Poor's-500 index in 1987.

smoothing average is eight days in both figures. Note the divergence between prices and Qstick in August: Qstick peaked before prices made a secondary, lower high in early October.

QSTICK AND MOMENTUM

Because Qstick is defined using a momentum calculation, there is a broad similarity between Qstick and momentum. Nevertheless, the two can diverge significantly based on market action. We illustrate this feature using the September, 1993 Coffee futures contract in Figure 4.4. We show the 8-day Qstick and momentum superimposed on one another. Qstick

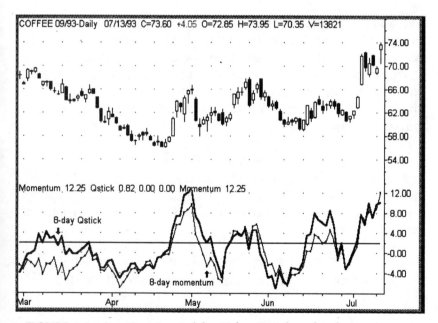

FIGURE 4.4 A comparison of the 8-day Qstick and 8-day momentum for the September, 1993 coffee contract. The heavy line is the Qstick and the thin line is the momentum.

and momentum diverge and converge depending on market action; specifically, they tend to converge when markets make trending moves, and diverge during sideways periods. Qstick often moves faster and farther than momentum.

When the open is near the prior day's close, then Qstick and momentum converge. Mathematically, the difference between today's close (C) and the open (O), $C-O$, is roughly equal to $C-C_1$, when yesterday's close, C_1, and today's open O are not far apart. This occurs during quiet periods in the market. When the open is far away from the prior close, then Qstick and momentum diverge. This divergence usually occurs in trending markets driven by external events.

Intraday Momentum Index

We noted that the difference between the close and the open is at the heart of candlestick analysis and quantified this difference using a simple moving average to get Qstick. Further, it would be useful to have an oscillator to pinpoint extremes in intraday momentum. We could develop such an oscillator, the intraday momentum index (IMI), by adapting the computational approach used in relative strength index (RSI) calculations.

Following the RSI approach, we separate the intraday momentum into bullish days and bearish days, getting positive numbers in both columns. We can then define an intraday momentum index (IMI) over, say, 14 days using the equation below:

IS_U = Sum of Intraday Momentum UP (C > O),

IS_D = Sum of Intraday Momentum Down (C < O),

$$IMI = \frac{IS_U}{(IS_U + IS_D)} * 100. \tag{4.2}$$

You no doubt recognize the similarity to the RSI. You can now gauge if white or black candles dominated recent market action. IMI values will be greater than 70 if white candles predominate. Conversely, IMI values will be below 20 if black bodies predominate. When the market is in a trading range, IMI values will be in the neutral range of 40 to 60.

As a market tries to bottom after a sell off, there are gradually more candles with white bodies, even though prices remain in a narrow range. We can detect this shift using the IMI, because its values will increase towards 70. Similarly, as a market begins to top, there will be more black candles, causing IMI values to decline towards 20. Therefore, IMI can be used to quantify subtle shifts in intraday momentum that usually precede changes in interday momentum. Thus, the IMI is another way to quantify candlesticks.

Notice, for example, the IMI for the deutsche mark March, 1993 contract in Figure 4.5. The internal momentum index peaked and bottomed shortly before closing prices.

In short, the IMI is useful because the intraday momentum differs from interday momentum (Qstick) at key turning points. As a result, we can use the IMI and Qstick together for a better understanding of price action.

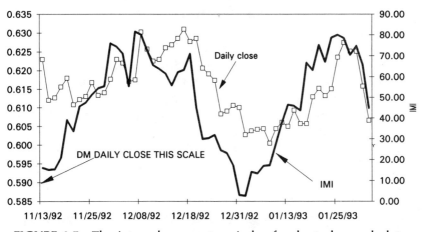

FIGURE 4.5 The internal momentum index for deutsche mark data.

QUANTIFYING CANDLESTICK SHADOWS

Just as we have quantified the candlestick body by defining Qstick and IMI, we can quantify the shadows of the candlestick patterns by separating the upper shadow and lower shadow for each day. This will highlight days with unusually long upper or lower shadows, a useful feature, since these are thought to occur near turning points. You can define the shadows as:

$$
\begin{aligned}
\text{upper shadow} &= \text{high} \ - \ \text{close (if close} > \text{open)}, \\
&= \text{high} \ - \ \text{open (if close} < \text{open)}, \qquad (4.3) \\
\text{lower shadow} &= \text{open} \ - \ \text{low} \ \ (\text{if close} > \text{open}), \\
&= \text{close} \ - \ \text{low} \ \ (\text{if close} < \text{open}).
\end{aligned}
$$

You can take a simple or exponential moving average of the daily upper and lower shadows to show the recent trend. Candlestick analysts have observed that, when a market is definite about its direction, it shows short shadows. Hence, when the moving average of the shadows is declining, we can be confident about market direction. However, when a market is unsure about its direction, it has long shadows. We can observe this indecision as an increase in the moving averages. To spot market indecision, follow the daily shadows and their moving averages.

Candlestick analysts have categorized the formations called hammer or hanging man by their long shadows. These are reversal patterns, and it is the length of the shadows that is more important than the color of the body. Subsequently, a plot of the upper and lower shadows will quickly identify days with unusually long shadows. You can then compare the lengths of the shadows to those at previous turning points.

The Treasury Bond market often shows long shadows. Figure 4.6 illustrates the candlestick chart for the 09/93 T-Bond contract along with the measured upper and lower tails plotted below. We have circled the interesting areas of the pattern. Note the long upper and lower shadows showing indecision

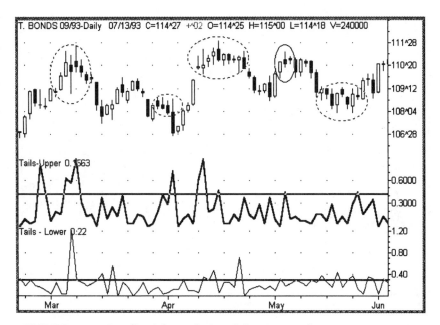

FIGURE 4.6 Candlestick analysis of the September, 1993, Treasury Bond futures contract, and a graph of the upper and lower shadows.

(or nearby resistance and support) in March. These shadows were much longer than usual, as shown by the lower graphs, warning of an intermediate top.

Also note the upper shadows showing local resistance in early April in this figure. When the market pushed through this resistance, it moved quickly to new highs. Once again, there was resistance near highs of March, as shown by the long upper shadows. The sideways movement produced large shadows, showing indecision. Similarly, the base formed in mid-to-late May also produced large lower shadows, showing nearby support.

The currency markets also show long shadows, as you can see in Figure 4.7 of the 09/93 deutsche mark contract. Long lower shadows show local support, whereas upper shadows show local resistance. Choppy sideways trading (such as late

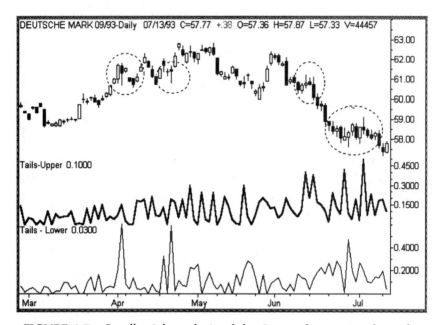

FIGURE 4.7   Candlestick analysis of the September, 1993, deutsche mark futures contract with upper and lower shadows plotted separately.

June and July) produced long shadows on both sides. For example, a long lower shadow showed support as the market bounced weakly; a long upper shadow showed resistance. The DM weakened after this long upper shadow, making new lows.

You can measure the upper and lower shadows and plot the measurements in graphs for trading decisions. A graph of the upper and lower shadows lets you compare today's shadows with recent market action to evaluate its significance. You could use the upper or lower shadows to find local resistance and support, selling near resistance and buying near the support, with a close stop to protect your position.

CASE IN POINT: ANALYZING THREE STOCKS WITH QSTICK

In this section you'll see applications of the Qstick idea to longer-term analysis of stock prices. These examples show how quantified candlesticks can improve your analysis of stock price action. Figure 4.8 shows a weekly chart of Amgen (AMGN) covering the period June, 1992 through June, 1993. The figure includes a 10-week simple moving average of the weekly close and a 5-week Qstick smoothed with a 5-week simple moving average.

Amgen rallied from mid-1991, peaking at 78¼ in early January, 1992. The broad top in Qstick in September, 1992 led to a sideways move into November. Then, Qstick bottomed and rose sharply into January. The Qstick peaked on 1/03/

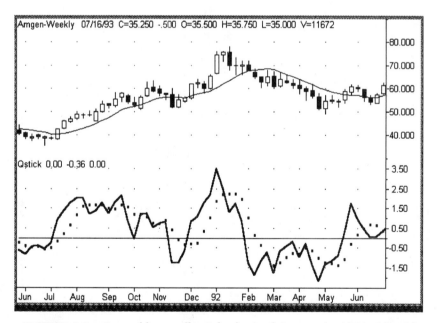

FIGURE 4.8 A weekly candlestick chart of Amgen in 1991–92 with a 5-week Qstick.

93, ahead of the actual peak in prices two weeks later. Qstick dropped below its own moving average the week of 1/17/92, when Amgen closed at 70. Thus, there was advance notice of a significant top in the sharp peak in Qstick and its decisive break below its own moving average. The sell signal was in force for three weeks before Amgen began its slide into April, 1993.

Figure 4.9 shows weekly Amgen data from July, 1992 through July, 1993. Note again the sharp peak in Qstick in the week of 11/13/92, before the stock peaked at 78 the week of 12/04/93. This was a double top in Amgen. The Qstick was decisively below its own moving average in January, 1993 before Amgen prices fell below the 10-week average and collapsed. Qstick bottomed with prices in March, and accelerated above its moving average close to the actual bottom in

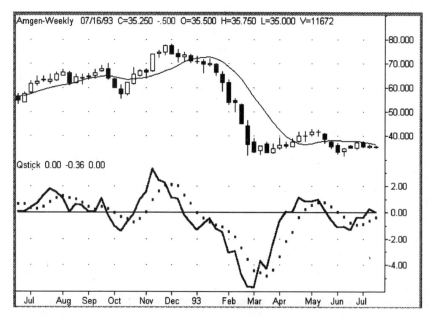

FIGURE 4.9   A weekly candlestick chart of Amgen in 1992–93 with a 5-week Qstick.

mid-March. This example shows that Qstick provides early warning of trend changes, particularly when the market makes sharp moves.

Qstick also proves valuable in analyzing longer moves, as you can see in Figure 4.10, a chart of weekly General Electric (GE) data from February, 1988 through November, 1990. This period includes the move following the October, 1987 crash into the next significant decline. We plotted the 30-week Qstick with its 30-week simple moving average. Note how the Qstick made a sharp peak on 6/1/90 and broke down the week of 8/3/90, well before the big slide in October. GE was at 69¾ when Qstick broke below its multiyear upward channel. The Qstick analysis provides a useful insight into the trend change in GE.

The GE analysis continues in Figure 4.11 covering July,

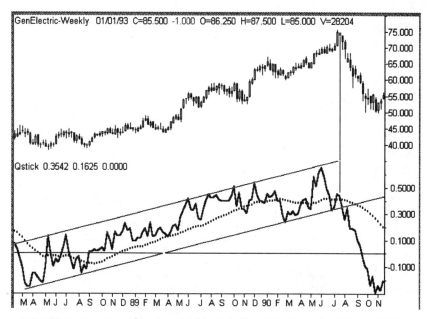

FIGURE 4.10   A multiyear weekly candlestick chart for General Electric along with a long-term Qstick and its moving average.

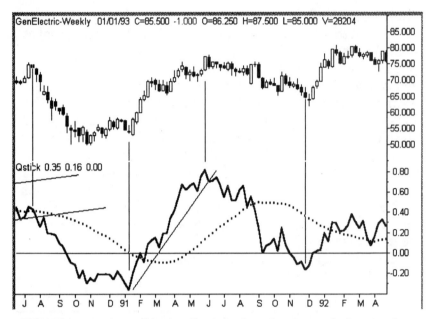

FIGURE 4.11   A weekly candlestick chart for General Electric along with a long-term Qstick.

1991 through April, 1992. This figure shows a 30-week Qstick smoothed by its 30-week moving average. A trend line analysis quickly reveals important changes. The key turning points occurred a bit before key moves in GE stock. From this, you can see that Qstick analysis can be used for long-term analysis of individual stocks.

Figure 4.11 also shows that Qstick can be used to confirm candlestick patterns. The bullish engulfing pattern in January, 1991, was confirmed by a bottom in Qstick. Similarly, the bullish morning star pattern in December, 1991 was confirmed by an uptick in Qstick. The peak in May, 1991, did not quite produce a dark cloud cover pattern; it did, however, occur near the top of the Qstick rally, and broke the uptrend line. Thus, the Qstick chart helped to clarify a potential top.

Finally, Figure 4.12 is example of intermediate term analysis using a 20-day Qstick and its 20-day moving average. We used Philip Morris (MO) daily data from its top in September, 1992 through May, 1993. The Qstick fell below its average in mid-September, signalling the coming top. The 20-day moving average turned negative in mid-October, suggesting lower prices to come. The 20-day average moved up to the zero line following the rally in mid-December. It stayed in negative territory all the way to late May, 1993. The Qstick also did not turn positive from the second week of December, 1992 through the first week of May, 1993. The Qstick indicator called the top in MO and stayed on the short side of the market throughout the decline. Using Qstick, you could have avoided a big decline in Philip Morris, or more than doubled your money with a short position.

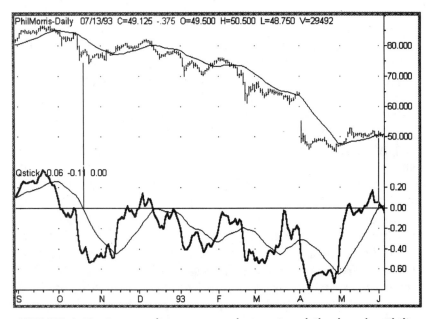

FIGURE 4.12 Intermediate-term analysis using daily data for Philip Morris with a 20-day Qstick and its 20-day simple moving average.

SUMMARY

The purpose of quantifying candlesticks is to improve identification of candlestick patterns. We quantified the patterns using the candle body, via Qstick (a moving average) and the internal momentum index (an oscillator). We also quantified the shadows by separating upper and lower shadows. These indicators can be used by themselves, or to clarify interpretation of candlestick patterns. We showed how these ideas can be used for short, intermediate, and long-term analysis of stocks or futures.

TUTORIAL ON QSTICK

Calculating Qstick

Table 4.1 shows data for the deutsche mark, March, 1993 contract. We did not use any decimal points in the data. The first day was 01/18/93 and the last day was 02/02/93. We calculated the daily Qstick value as the difference between the close and the open; in the last column we have taken a 5-day simple moving average of the daily Qstick values, but you can change the number of days as you wish.

Let's assume you are a trend follower. You would then go short on day 11 since the Qstick value had crossed 0 and become negative on day 10. But what if you were an aggressive trader? Then, you would take the sum of daily (C−O) changes at the start of day 10. This sum is 35 ticks (+59−27−7+10); hence, you recognize that if DM closed 35 ticks or more below the open, that would push Qstick below 0. You could plan a short sale, say, 40 ticks below the open of day 10. Thus, you could have sold short on day 10 at the 6,209 level. Your profit would have been over $2,100 on this trade over the next two days.

Table 4.1 Sample Qstick Calculations with Deutsche Mark, March 1993 Contract

Day	Open (O)	High	Low	Close (C)	Daily (C−O)	Qstick 5-day Average
1	6063	6162	6057	6153	90	
2	6151	6176	6129	6163	12	
3	6152	6191	6152	6185	33	
4	6185	6207	6132	6149	−36	
5	6155	6053	6151	6241	86	37.00
6	6241	6322	6235	6300	59	30.80
7	6295	6338	6274	6288	−7	27.00
8	6287	6290	6251	6260	−27	15.00
9	6256	6314	6251	6266	10	24.20
10	6249	6281	6158	6168	−81	−9.20
11	6166	6173	6066	6071	−95	−40.00
12	6071	6105	6038	6055	−16	−41.80

Table 4.2 Sample Calculations for IMI Using Deutsche Mark Data

Open (O)	Close (C)	Up Day (C−O)	Down Day (C−O)	5-Day Sum of Up Day (E)	5-Day Sum of Down Day (F)	Sum of Up & Down Day (G)	IMI= E/G *100
6063	6153	90	0				
6151	6163	12	0				
6152	6185	33	0				
6185	6149	0	36				
6155	6241	86	0	221	36	257	85.99
6241	6300	59	0	190	36	226	84.07
6295	6288	0	7	178	43	221	80.54
6287	6260	0	27	145	70	215	67.44
6256	6266	10	0	155	34	189	82.01
6249	6168	0	81	69	115	184	37.50
6166	6071	0	95	10	210	220	4.55
6071	6055	0	16	10	219	229	4.37

Calculating IMI

Let's look at IMI calculations using deutsche mark data (see Table 4.2). We first separate the daily $(C-O)$ difference into up and down days. On up days, the market closed higher than the open; on down days the market closed below the open. We show a 5-day sum of the up-day (column E) and down-day (column F) intraday momentum. Then we show the sum of those momentum numbers (Column G). The IMI is simply the ratio of columns E and G.

5
New Momentum Oscillators

A large group of technical indicators falls into the general category of momentum oscillators, which show market momentum over a fixed time period on a fixed scale. We examined many such momentum indicators in Chapter 1, such as the relative strength index (RSI), the stochastic oscillator, and the commodity channel index. The differences in these indicators arise out of their definition, the smoothing scheme and scaling approach.

Regardless of their differences, these oscillators have the following limitations in common:

- None of them is a "pure" momentum oscillator that measures momentum directly.
- The time period of the calculations is fixed, giving a different picture of market action for different time periods.
- They all mirror the price pattern; hence, you may benefit more by directly trading prices themselves.
- They do not consistently show extremes in prices because they use a constant time period.

- The smoothing mechanism introduces lags and obscures short-term price extremes that are actually valuable for trading.

This chapter introduces a package of oscillators that addresses and mitigates the weaknesses of the RSI and other widely used momentum oscillators.

CHANDE MOMENTUM OSCILLATOR

One of the most powerful measures of price evolution is momentum, defined as the difference between today's close and some previous close. The Chande momentum oscillator (CMO), introduced in the previous chapter, is a pure momentum oscillator that plots momentum on a bounded scale. It helps to spot extremes in market momentum, and you'll see that it has many uses in technical analysis. The CMO is a variant of the RSI, but differs from it in the following ways:

1. It directly measures momentum, because it uses data for both up and down days in its numerator. The RSI uses data for up days only in its numerator.
2. It does not use built-in smoothing in its calculations, and hence does not obscure short-lived extremes in momentum. Calculations are performed on unsmoothed data, then, once calculated, CMO values can be smoothed like any other indicator. The RSI has built-in smoothing (calculations are performed on smoothed data), which has a great effect on its values.
3. It varies from -100 to $+100$, so you can see net market momentum at a glance on a bounded scale. RSI varies from 0 to 100, so you must use the 50 level to assess net market momentum.

You can more clearly see the differences between CMO and RSI in the following definitions:

Chande momentum ocillator $= 100^*(S_u - S_d)/(S_u + S_d)$
unsmoothed RSI $= 100^*(S_u/(S_u + S_d))$ (5.1)

Here, S_u is the sum of up-day momentum over x days, and S_d is the sum of down-day momentum over x days. (Refer to the tutorial on RSI for a detailed look at these quantities.) The CMO numerator has the difference between the up-day momentum and down-day momentum. The numerator is actually the x-day momentum because the values of S_u and S_d are not smoothed before being used for the CMO calculations. The denominator gives the indicator its bounded scale. Consequently, CMO is a net momentum oscillator.

The RSI calculations smooth S_u and S_d before they are used to calculate today's RSI value. This built-in smoothing mechanism has a great influence on the actual RSI values, because it often obscures short-lived extremes in momentum. This is an important difference between CMO and RSI. We will clarify these ideas by showing sample CMO and RSI calculations using T-Bond or S&P-500 data.

CMO Calculations: T-Bond Data

Let's use daily T-Bond 06/93 contract data and begin by calculating the up-day and down-day daily momentum. Next, we calculate the 10-day sum of the up-day momentum (S_u) and down day momentum (S_d). We calculate the 10-day CMO using Equation 5.1. Using the data from Table 5.1, we show the calculation of the first two values as:

$$CMO_1 = 100^*(2.0937-0.375)/(2.0937+0.375) = 69.62,$$
$$CMO_2 = 100^*(2.25-.375)/(2.25+0.375) = 71.43. \quad (5.2)$$

We use the subscripts 1 and 2 to indicate the first and second days. Note that we did not smooth the daily totals for S_u and S_d. We prefer to calculate CMO with unsmoothed totals. You

Table 5.1 Calculating 10-day CMO Using T-Bond 06/93 Data

Close	Up-Mtm	Dn-Mtm	S(u)	S(d)	10-Day
			Up-Mtm 10-Day Total	Dn-Mtm 10-Day Total	CMO
101.0313					
101.0313	0	0			
101.125	0.0937	0			
101.9687	0.8437	0			
102.7813	0.8126	0			
103	0.2187	0			
102.9687	0	0.0313			
103.0625	0.0938	0			
102.9375	0	0.125			
102.7188	0	0.2187			
102.75	0.0312	0	2.0937	0.375	69.62
102.9063	0.1563	0	2.25	0.375	71.43
102.9687	0.0624	0	2.2187	0.375	71.08

can then smooth the CMO values using a simple or exponential moving average.

A better way to visualize the CMO is to rewrite it in terms of relative and absolute momentum. Relative momentum is the daily signed momentum, and is given by the difference of today's close and yesterday's close:

$$CMO = 100 * (Momentum)/(|Momentum|). \qquad (5.3)$$

The CMO simply shows the net momentum as a fraction of the absolute momentum changes over the desired time period. This is another reason for calling CMO a pure momentum oscillator. If the market moves up or down for several days, CMO will be positive or negative. You can then tell at a glance if the market action is one-sided. This is a useful feature, since it is also a measure of trendiness of the closing price. A market that is trending strongly has a high CMO value. We defined CMO using closing prices, but you also can calculate a CMO using daily highs, lows, or opening prices.

RSI Calculations: S&P-500 Index

Let's illustrate the impact of the smoothing scheme on indicator values by showing 14-day RSI calculations, in Table 5.2, using daily closing data for the S&P-500 index. Figure 5.1 also shows the daily close for the S&P-500 index and uses a portion of these data in Table 5.2. Note the particular pattern of closing prices for the index, especially the sequence of closes and their positions relative to one another, because we'll refer to them later.

Table 5.2 shows the up-day and down-day momentum. The up-day momentum is 0 if today's close is less than yesterday's; otherwise, it is the absolute difference between the two closes.

The down-day momentum is zero if today's close is greater than yesterday's close; otherwise, it is the absolute difference between the two closes.

The next two columns have the 14-day sum of the up-day (S_u) and down-day (S_d) momentum. Figure 5.2 shows the unsmoothed 14-day sum of up-day and down-day momentum. Notice that these lines also show price extremes. The two lines cross one another when the net momentum over 14 days $\pm$. When the 14-day net momentum is positive, the line representing the up-day sum (S_u) is above the down-day sum (S_d). The reverse is true when the 14-day net momentum is negative. The CMO shows precisely this relationship, since the numerator is the difference between $S_u - S_d$.

The RSI calculations, described by J. Welles Wilder, Jr. in his book *New Concepts in Technical Trading Systems*, smooth the S_u and S_d data from day 2 forward. This smoothing adds 1/14 of the new value to 13/14ths of the previous value of these variables, which amounts to roughly a 27-day exponential moving average.

Table 5.2   RSI Calculations for S&P-500 Index

Date	S&P-500 Close	Up-Day Mtm	Dn-Day Mtm	14-Day Up Sum	Down Sum	RSI Smth	RSI UnSm
01/04/93	435.380						
01/05/93	434.340	0.00	1.04				
01/06/93	434.520	0.18	0.00				
01/07/93	430.730	0.00	3.79				
01/08/93	429.050	0.00	1.68				
01/11/93	430.950	1.90	0.00				
01/12/93	431.040	0.09	0.00				
01/13/93	433.030	1.99	0.00				
01/14/93	435.940	2.91	0.00				
01/15/93	437.150	1.21	0.00				
01/18/93	436.840	0.00	0.31				
01/19/93	435.130	0.00	1.71				
01/20/93	433.370	0.00	1.76				
01/21/93	435.490	2.12	0.00				
01/22/93	436.110	0.62	0.00	0.79	0.74	51.71	51.71
01/25/93	440.010	3.90	0.00	1.01	0.68	59.66	61.73
01/26/93	439.950	0.00	0.06	0.94	0.64	59.50	61.29
01/27/93	438.110	0.00	1.84	0.87	0.72	54.60	66.70
01/28/93	438.660	0.55	0.00	0.85	0.67	55.77	72.91
01/29/93	438.780	0.12	0.00	0.80	0.62	56.04	70.40
02/01/93	442.520	3.74	0.00	1.01	0.58	63.44	75.13
02/02/93	442.550	0.03	0.00	0.94	0.54	63.50	72.80
02/03/93	447.200	4.65	0.00	1.20	0.50	70.62	74.89
02/04/93	449.560	2.36	0.00	1.28	0.46	73.46	76.10
02/05/93	448.930	0.00	0.63	1.19	0.48	71.48	75.09

We used the smoothed values of S_u and S_d for RSI calculations and unsmoothed values of S_u and S_d for CMO. This is the critical difference between RSI and CMO. The other important difference is in the numerator: The RSI uses just the up-day sum, S_u, whereas CMO uses the x day momentum,

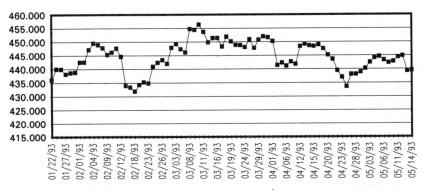

FIGURE 5.1   Daily close of the S&P-500 index.

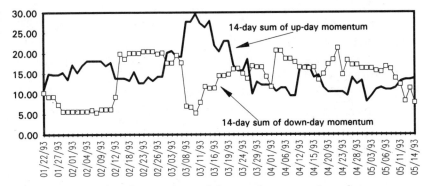

FIGURE 5.2   This shows plots of the 14-day sum of up-day momentum and down-day momentum for the S&P-500 index data in Figure 5.1.

given by ($S_u - S_d$). For example, on 1/25/93, the smoothed values of S_u and S_d are calculated as follows (see Table 5.2):

$$S_u = (0.79*13+3.90)/14 = 1.0121,$$
$$S_d = (0.74*13+0)/14 = 0.6871, \qquad (5.4)$$
$$RSI = 100*(1.0121/(1.0121+0.6871)) = 59.56.$$

The 01/25/93 value of RSI in Table 5.2 is 59.66. The difference between our sample RSI value of 59.56 and the tabulated value is caused by the rounding of the numbers.

Figure 5.3 shows the 14-day smoothed RSI and the 14-day unsmoothed RSI (RSI*). Notice how the RSI looks similar to the price changes (price pattern) of the S&P-500 index. The RSI* differs markedly from the RSI. It looks more like momentum, as you will see below. Note how the RSI* was above 80 in March, even though the RSI barely reached 70. Your trading decisions would be quite different in the two instances, which highlights the importance of smoothing in indicator design.

Figure 5.4 shows the 14-day unsmoothed CMO and the 14-day RSI. Note that there are significant differences in the appearance of the two curves, even though CMO and the RSI* are related, since CMO = 2 * RSI* − 100. You can clearly see this similarity by comparing the appearance of the CMO in Figure 5.4 with the RSI* in Figure 5.3.

Figure 5.5 plots the 14-day momentum of the S&P-500 index over the same time period as in Figures 5.3 and 5.4.

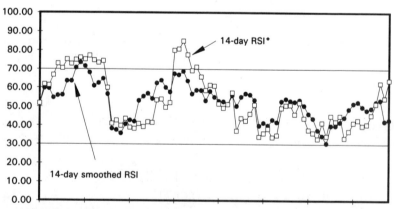

FIGURE 5.3 A comparison of the 14-day smoothed and unsmoothed values of the RSI for the S&P-500 index data in Figure 5.1.

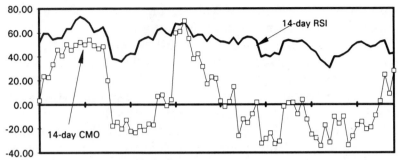

FIGURE 5.4   A comparison of the 14-day smoothed RSI and the 14-day CMO.

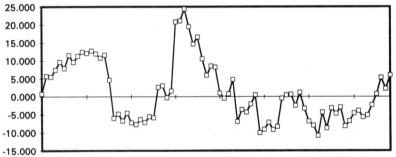

FIGURE 5.5   The 14-day momentum for the S&P-500 index data in Figure 5.1.

The momentum figure is identical (except for scaling) to the unsmoothed CMO. However, the momentum calculation ($C_0 - C_x$) is, by definition, unbounded. Hence, we cannot readily transform momentum into a bounded oscillator. But, this is precisely the advantage of the CMO definition. Figure 5.4 shows that unsmoothed CMO is a "pure" momentum oscillator that plots momentum on a bounded scale from $+100$ to -100 (or $+1$ to -1).

Next we'll show the effect of varying the length of the

smoothing period on RSI values. Figure 5.6 compares the effect of a 9-day exponential smoothing versus the traditional 27-day smoothing. Using 70 and 30 as reference values for overbought and oversold conditions, the lightly smoothed RSI reached price extremes more often than the heavily smoothed version. For example, the 9-day smoothed RSI was overbought in January and severely oversold in April. The 27-day smoothed RSI barely nudged 70 and 30 at that same time. Thus, your interpretation of RSI would change significantly as smoothing changes. And, because the CMO does not have any built-in smoothing, it could show price extremes that RSI may not.

We'll show you some actual numbers to show how smoothing makes a difference to RSI values. Table 5.3 shows the details of the RSI calculations with a 9-day exponential moving average (index = 0.20). For this example, look at the calculations for 01/25/93:

$$S_u = 0.2*3.9+0.8*0.79 = 1.412 = 1.41,$$
$$S_d = 0.2*0 + 0.8*0.74 = 0.592 = 0.59, \qquad (5.5)$$
$$RSI = 100*(1.41/(1.41+0.59)) = 70.50.$$

The difference from the tabulated value of 70.57 is a result

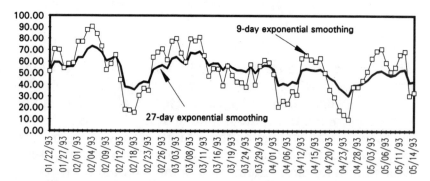

FIGURE 5.6 A chart of RSI values with the usual 27-day exponential smoothing and a short 9-day exponential smoothing.

Table 5.3 RSI Calculations with 9-day Exponential Moving Average

Date	S&P-500 Close	Up-Day Mtm	Dn-Day Mtm	S(u) ← Smoothed →	S(d)	RSI
01/04/93	435.380					
01/05/93	434.340	0.00	1.04			
01/06/93	434.520	0.18	0.00			
01/07/93	430.730	0.00	3.79			
01/08/93	429.050	0.00	1.68			
01/11/93	430.950	1.90	0.00			
01/12/93	431.040	0.09	0.00			
01/13/93	433.030	1.99	0.00			
01/14/93	435.940	2.91	0.00			
01/15/93	437.150	1.21	0.00			
01/18/93	436.840	0.00	0.31			
01/19/93	435.130	0.00	1.71			
01/20/93	433.370	0.00	1.76			
01/21/93	435.490	2.12	0.00			
01/22/93	436.110	0.62	0.00	0.79	0.74	51.71
01/25/93	440.010	3.90	0.00	1.41	0.59	70.57
01/26/93	439.950	0.00	0.06	1.13	0.48	70.04
01/27/93	438.110	0.00	1.84	0.90	0.75	54.48
01/28/93	438.660	0.55	0.00	0.83	0.60	57.97
01/29/93	438.780	0.12	0.00	0.69	0.48	58.83
02/01/93	442.520	3.74	0.00	1.30	0.39	77.10
02/02/93	442.550	0.03	0.00	1.05	0.31	77.20

of the rounding to two decimal places. The unsmoothed RSI* value is 61.73, as shown in Table 5.2. The RSI value is 59.66 with a 27-day exponential smoothing. This smoothing often obscures short-lived market extremes, which may mean the difference between closing a position or reversing it, closing it at a smaller profit, or even a loss.

Because there is no built-in smoothing in the CMO calculations, you can obtain a smoother indicator by increasing the number of days in the CMO calculations. For instance, by choosing, say, a 14-day time frame, we will have a smoother CMO curve versus a 9-day time frame. Figure 5.7 illustrates this idea by showing a 9-day and 14-day CMO for the S&P-500 index. Then, when the 9-day CMO is overlaid on the daily close of the index in Figure 5.8, you can see that it was more volatile than the 14-day CMO. The 9-day CMO clearly showed price extremes in the index by rising above 0.70 or falling below −0.70. The 14-day CMO in Figure 5.7 did not show the price extremes as obviously. Thus, you could use the 9-day CMO for short-term trading of the S&P-500 index.

CMO as Measure of Trendiness

One of the useful features of the CMO is that it can also be used as a measure of trendiness, and trendiness measures are very important because you can use them to open trend-following trades when they confirm the presence of a trend. We discussed trendiness in some detail in Chapter 2 on linear regression, and we'll use a trendiness measure—vertical hor-

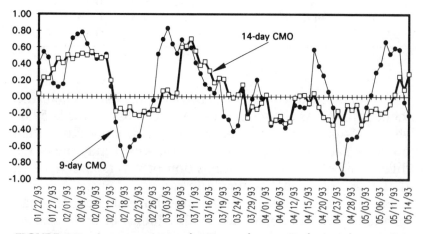

FIGURE 5.7 A comparison of using a shorter (9-day) or longer (14-day) interval to calculate the CMO.

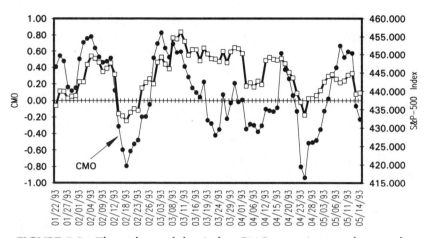

FIGURE 5.8 The values of the 9-day CMO superimposed upon the S&P-500 daily close.

izontal filter (VHF)—from that chapter for our test of the CMO.

First, we'll compare the definitions of VHF and CMO to point out some similarities between them. In the definition of VHF below, let R be the range over x days, where R = H − L, H being the highest high and L being the lowest low. Let P_n be the sum of the absolute value of the daily close-to-close changes (momentum) over the x days. We now define VHF as:

$$VHF = R/P_n. \tag{5.6}$$

In calculating CMO and RSI, we separated the daily close-to-close changes into those for up days and down days. We can take the sum of those changes over x days to get (S_u + S_d). You will recognize that P_n is essentially equal to (S_u + S_d).

At key turning points, the close is not far from the highest high or lowest low of the period. Thus, to a good approximation, we can replace the range, R, with the absolute difference $|(C_0 - C_x)|$, the momentum of the close taken over x days. When the market makes a swing move, today's close could be at one extreme, and the close, x days ago, at the other. The momentum of the close could then be very close to the actual range.

In effect, the absolute value of CMO is similar in construction to the VHF and should be a good indicator of trendiness. The denominator is essentially the same, and the numerator will tend to converge at key turning points. We already verified this during the discussion on linear regression analysis, where we found that the smoothed VHF, r^2 and absolute CMO (absCMO) were excellent indicators of trendiness.

In Figure 5.9 we compared a 14-day VHF to the 14-day unsmoothed absolute CMO. The calculations are for the S&P-500 index data used earlier. We used the absolute values of CMO (absCMO) since the VHF has only positive values. Notice how absCMO and VHF converge at a key turning point in early March. There are differences in the absCMO and VHF because the CMO uses momentum rather than the range in the numerator.

The VHF falls as the market enters into a period of congestion; that is, the range narrows. The denominator of the VHF is a scaling reference; the numerator, or range, determines the

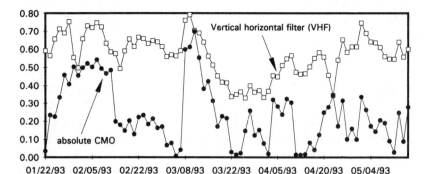

FIGURE 5.9 A comparison of the 14-day VHF and the 14-day absolute CMO for the S&P-500 index data.

value of VHF. The price range can widen without rising momentum, because of small progress on a closing basis. The VHF will show trendiness when absCMO does not. Thus, we can say absCMO is a measure of trendiness on a closing basis.

The fact that absolute momentum shows trendiness is reinforced in Figure 5.10, which used weekly data for GE. We have plotted the absolute 10-week momentum and its 5-week simple moving average. Note how the absolute momentum increases during a rapid move in prices and falls when prices enter a trading range. Also notice how momentum was flat all through the trading range in 1992. The momentum peaks at different values each time because its scale is not fixed.

In short, absolute momentum, and therefore absCMO, can be used to measure trendiness in data just like VHF. When these indicators show that a trend exists, you can put on trend-following positions with greater confidence of success.

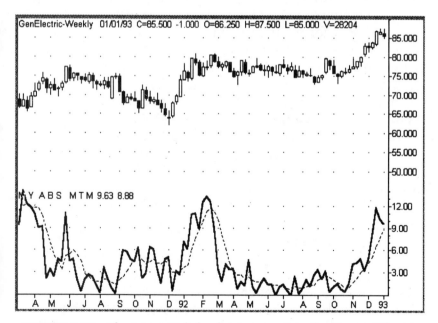

FIGURE 5.10 The 14-period absolute momentum for General Electric using weekly data.

Useful Features of CMO

The beauty of the CMO approach is that it converts momentum into an oscillator that you can plot on a fixed scale. By using absCMO to plot the absolute momentum on a bounded scale from 0 to 100, you can get a consistent scale to compare different market moves.

You can also use CMO to define overbought and oversold levels at +50 and −50 where the ratio of S_u to S_d is 3:1 or 1:3. By simple substitution you can find that a ratio of 3:1 corresponds to a value of +50. This means that the up-day momentum is three times the down-day momentum, a rare occurrence. The reverse is also true; if the up-day momentum is only one third of the down-day momentum, then this oscillator has a value of −50.

Another convenient feature of CMO is that we get positive and negative values. Hence, we can tell if the net market action is falling or rising. Figure 5.11 shows a 14-day RSI and 14-day CMO for a direct comparison using the July, 1993 Wheat contract. The reference levels for CMO (upper indicator) are +60 and −60, and they correspond to RSI values of 80 and 20. Note how the CMO stayed in negative territory during the downtrend in prices from mid-January through March. The divergence between the CMO and prices as the market made new lows in June was a harbinger of the rally in July. The RSI did not show any significant market extremes during this period, nor did it show a significant divergence with the price as the contract made new lows.

In addition to RSI, we can compare CMO to other indicators and find new uses for it. For instance, CMO resembles both the true strength index (TSI) and the average directional index (ADX). But, as you'll see, gives us additional information. The TSI, described by William Blau, uses doubly smoothed exponential averages for the relative and absolute momentum. Hence, its values differ significantly from the CMO and will show greater sensitivity to price changes. On the other hand, because of the exponential smoothing, the

FIGURE 5.11   A comparison of the 14-day unsmoothed CMO to the RSI using the September, 1993 CBT wheat futures contract.

TSI rarely approaches extremes of −100 and +100. Consequently, the CMO can show the extremes more readily. The choice of CMO or TSI will depend on your trading horizon and your preference for indicator sensitivity.

In Figure 5.12, you can see that the average absolute value of the smoothed CMO closely tracks the ADX of the directional movement system. The ADX is the thin line, and the averaged absolute CMO is the thick line. We used the September, 1993 US Bond contract to show the similarity between the 14-period ADX and the 14-period averaged absolute CMO. These indicators rose when the market was trending, and declined when the market was going sideways. Both indicators measure trendiness, but the absCMO was more responsive than the ADX in this example.

The ADX is a popular measure of trendiness in data. Many

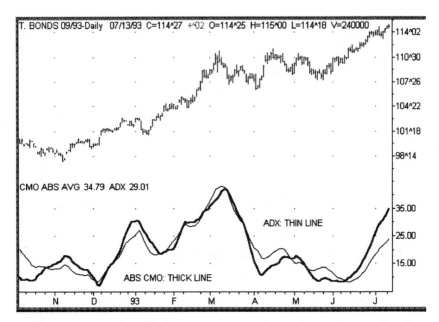

FIGURE 5.12   The absolute CMO and the 14-period ADX for the September, 1993 T-Bond contract.

traders use it to verify that a trend is underway or about to end. If you use the CMO and its absolute values, you can use a single indicator to do the work of many.

Volatility-Based Composite CMO

In the foregoing CMO calculations, we used a fixed time period, but you can overcome this limitation by combining the CMO values from several time periods to define a single, composite CMO. One approach is simply to average CMO values from different time periods without changing the relative weights. Alternately, you can use a volatility-based weighting to have a truly market-sensitive composite CMO. We will use the June, 1993 T-Bond contract to explain these ideas (see Figure 5.13 for the daily close).

FIGURE 5.13   The daily close of the June, 1993 Treasury Bond futures contract.

We calculated the CMO as usual, using 5, 10, and 20 day-time intervals. We chose these lengths arbitrarily, using popular round numbers. You can see all three CMO lines in Figure 5.14. The 5-day CMO is the most volatile, and easily reaches values of $+1$ and -1. This happens when there are five up days or down days in a row. The 20-day CMO is the smoothest curve, showing the least volatility. The 10-day CMO has a volatility between that of the 5- and 20-day CMO.

Different time periods are better suited to meet the needs of certain types of traders. The 5-day CMO and its volatility may suit a short-term trader, while the 10- and 20-day CMO volatility may suit an intermediate-term trader. The frequency of sign changes decreases as the time period increases, which just means that there is more smoothing in the data as the calculation period increases.

You can achieve a more sensitive alternative to the 20-day CMO by calculating the average CMO_A. This is simply an arithmetic average of the three values and is plotted in Figure 5.15. The 5-, 10- and 20-day CMO values are designated as CMO_5, CMO_{10} and CMO_{20}. As a result:

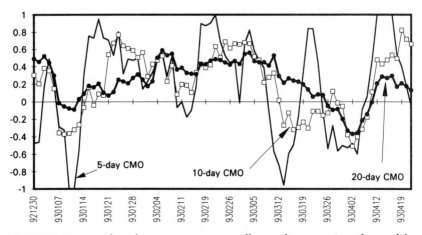

FIGURE 5.14   Chande momentum oscillator shown using three different time horizons for the T-Bond data in Figure 5.13: 5 days, 10 days and 20 days.

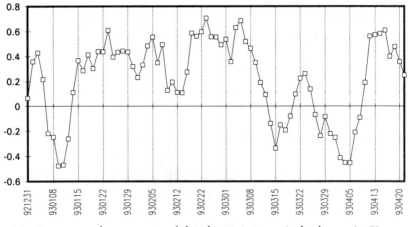

FIGURE 5.15   The average of the three time periods shown in Figure 5.14.

$$CMO_A = ((CMO_5 + CMO_{10} + CMO_{20})/3). \qquad (5.7)$$

and each has an equal weight (of 1/3) compared with the others.

This average CMO_A gives you a composite view of CMO over different time periods. You can combine other time periods as you desire. You would buy when the CMO turned positive, and sell when the CMO turned negative. This strategy would have worked well in this trending T-Bond market.

For an even more sensitive composite CMO, look at the volatility-weighted CMO in Figure 5.16. First, find the 5-day standard deviation of the 5-, 10- and 20-day CMO, calling the respective standard deviations S_1, S_2 and S_3. Then, define the volatility-weighted CMO_V by using them as the weights:

$$CMO_V = (S_1{}^* CMO_5 + S_2{}^* CMO_{10} \qquad (5.8)$$
$$+ S_3{}^* CMO_{20})/(S_1 + S_2 + S_3).$$

The volatility-weighted CMO_V is more sensitive to market action than CMO_A. Furthermore, CMO_V leads CMO_A at key

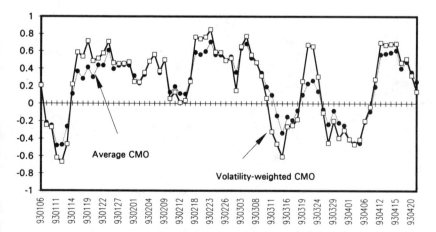

FIGURE 5.16 A comparison of the average composite CMO shown in Figure 5.15 with a volatility-weighted composite CMO.

crossings if the market moves rapidly. It also reaches a higher or lower extreme than the CMO_A. When CMO_V reaches a more extreme value than the CMO_A, a market reversal may be near. Using CMO_V is a way to include multiple time frames and market volatility in the analysis of market momentum.

Trading CMO with a Moving Average

To generate trading signals, you can use the CMO with its simple moving average (SMA). (Figure 5.17 shows the 10 day CMO with its 10 day SMA.) This approach allows you to initiate a trade before a zero crossing of the CMO. Be aware, however, that it sometimes gives early signals. You could buy when the CMO crossed above its average, and sell when it fell below its moving average. Such an approach would have a given a good entry point in January, 1993 at the start of the rally. However, the short signal in early February was premature; the market went sideways and lost some upward momentum. The loss of momentum pushed the CMO below

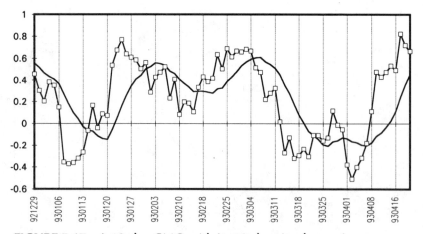

FIGURE 5.17 A 10-day CMO with its 10-day simple moving average. The T-bond data used to calculate CMO are in Figure 5.13.

its average, triggering the sell signal. The same approach would have put you back into the market, on the long side, 11 days later, but you would have missed a part of the move from 106 to 108.

Filtering Trading Noise from CMO

So far we have used the daily momentum change in our CMO even when the market moved by a small amount. Hence, some of the daily noise of trading creeps into the indicator. By filtering the CMO to ignore small changes in daily momentum, you will be better able to focus on the big picture.

One way to filter the noise is to use the daily difference in the CMO calculations *only* if it exceeds a threshold value. For example, consider the actively traded Treasury Bond futures contract. Assume that a daily closing difference of 2 ticks $(2/32 = 0.0625)$, or less, signals an unchanged market. We then can set the daily momentum (whether up or down) to 0 if the change is "small." We can show the difference in approach as follows:

$$
\begin{aligned}
\text{Mtm(up)} &= C_0 - C_1, & \text{if } C_0 - C_1 \text{ (unfiltered)}, \\
&= 0 & \text{if } C_0 < C_1, & \qquad (5.8) \\
\text{Mtm(up,f)} &= C_0 - C_1, & \text{if } (C_0 - C_1) > x \text{ (filtered)}, \\
&= 0 & \text{if } (C_0 - C_1) <= x.
\end{aligned}
$$

You can write similar equations for down-day momentum, and choose x arbitrarily. Or, you can use 100 days data to find average values for daily momentum changes on up days and down days. If you find the standard deviation of those daily changes over 100 days, you can use the average change plus one standard deviation as the value of x in the above filter. This approach can ignore some seemingly large values.

In Figure 5.18 you can view the CMO calculated with and without filtering, using the same data as in Figures 5.13

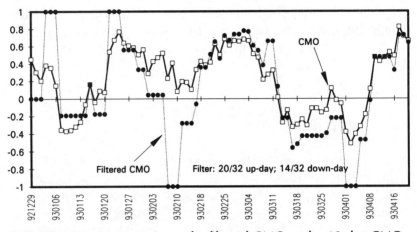

FIGURE 5.18   A comparison of a filtered CMO and a 10-day CMO.

through 5.17. We calculated the filter using 100 days data and the average plus one standard deviation of the daily momentum changes. The filter for up-day momentum was 20/32 and 14/32 for down-day momentum. This means that, if the daily change on up days was less than or equal to 20/32, then that day's up momentum was set to 0. Similarly, if the down move was less than or equal to 14/32, the down-day momentum was set to 0. The daily momentum equation is as follows:

$$\text{up-day mtm} = \text{if}(\ (C_0 - C_1) > 20/32, (C_0 - C_1), 0),$$
$$\text{down-day mtm} = \text{if}(\ (C_1 - C_0) > 14/32, (C_1 - C_0), 0).$$
$$(5.9)$$

Here, C_0 is today's close and C_1 is yesterday's close.

Note in Figure 5.18 how the filtered CMO identified two key overbought positions and two key oversold conditions in the market. You can see that the two CMO calculations converge when the market makes big or significant moves. The filtered CMO flattens when the market makes small moves in a short-lived trading range. It also gives a clearer picture of market action when used with the unfiltered CMO.

Zero crossing of both types of CMO were significant. The early warning of market extremes provided by the filtered CMO would have been useful to some traders. The amount of the filter was set for intermediate-term trading, but you can experiment with different amounts of filtering.

We will explain the calculation of the filtered CMO using the data in Table 5.4. We set the filters at 5/32 for the T-Bond data for both the up-day and down-day momentum. In columns 2 and 3, we show the usual calculation of up-day and down-day momentum. If today's close is higher than yesterday's, then the up-day momentum is the difference between the two closes. If today's close is less than yesterday's, then

Table 5.4 Calculating 10-Day Filtered CMO

Close	Up Mtm	Dn Mtm	Filtered Up Mtm (5/32)	Filtered Dn Mtm (5/32)	Filtered 10-day CMO	Regular 10-day CMO
101.03						
101.03	0	0	0	0		
101.13	0.0937	0	0	0		
101.97	0.8437	0	0.8437	0		
102.78	0.8126	0	0.8126	0		
103.00	0.2187	0	0.2187	0		
102.97	0	0.0313	0	0		
103.06	0.0938	0	0	0		
102.94	0	0.125	0	0		
102.72	0	0.2187	0	0.2187		
102.75	0	0	0	0	0.79	0.69
102.91	0.1563	0	0.1563	0	0.81	0.71
102.97	0.0624	0	0	0	0.81	0.71
103.13	0.1563	0	0.1563	0	0.72	0.60
103.72	0.5938	0	0.5938	0	0.67	0.55
104.22	0.5	0	0.5	0	0.73	0.61

the up-day momentum is 0. A similar logic applies to the down-day momentum.

In columns 4 and 5, we added a filter to the daily momentum calculations. If today's close is greater than yesterday's close by 5/32 or more, then the up-day momentum is the difference between the two closes. If, however, today's close is higher than yesterday's close by less than 5/32 of a point, then we set today's up-day momentum equal to 0. We assume that the change is not significant if it is less than 5/32. As before, if today's close is less than yesterday's close, then the up-day momentum is also 0.

For example, on day 3, the up-day momentum was 0.09375, or 3/32. Since this is less than 5/32, we set the filtered up-day momentum equal to 0. Here we treat an upward close by 3 ticks in the bond market as "no change" on a trading basis. The same logic applies to down-day momentum. The up-day and down-day filters can be different, and could be based on market volatility. The filtering process is a way to reduce noise in the daily momentum calculations.

CMO Summary

As you have seen, the CMO is a flexible and versatile momentum oscillator that you can easily adapt to a variety of trading styles. In sum, you can:

- Use CMO to identify overbought or oversold conditions.
- Use CMO as a trendiness indicator.
- Combine CMO with a moving average to generate trading signals.
- Use CMO with a different amount of smoothing for trading.
- Combine CMO values calculated for different time periods into a composite CMO.
- Filter the CMO to ignore small changes in market values.

In short, CMO is one indicator that can do the job of many.

TUTORIAL: DEFINING RSI

In technical analysis we define momentum as the difference between two prices. The time period between the two prices varies; they can be as little as one period apart, where the period can be any time length from minutes to months. Most commonly, we use one trading day as the unit of time. With a one-day time period, the closing prices define momentum as shown below:

$$\text{momentum} = C(\text{today}) - C(\text{yesterday}). \qquad (5.10)$$

Since today's close can be above or below yesterday's close, momentum can be positive or negative. We will call this "relative momentum." We can define "absolute momentum," in which we ignore the sign of the daily momentum, as

$$|\text{momentum}| = |C(\text{today}) - C(\text{yesterday})|. \qquad (5.11)$$

The values of absolute momentum are always positive, while the values of relative momentum can be positive or negative. Let's do a small exercise. Consider five trading days using values for the S&P-500 index from 11/29/91 to 12/15/ 91. Now, let's calculate the daily relative momentum and absolute momentum. The calculations are shown in Table 5.5.

Note that the sum of the relative momentum over four days is equal to the momentum over four days. This occurs because the intermediate terms cancel each other when we add them. In the equation below, subscripts refer to the number of days back from today (0):

$$(C_0 - C_4) = (C_0 - C_1) + (C_1 - C_2) + (C_2 - C_3) + (C_3 - C_4)$$

We can continue this exercise in a modified format by separating the daily momentum into values for days when the market closes up or closes down. In each instance, the momentum values will be positive. On an up day, the momentum is today's close minus yesterday's close. On down days, momentum is yesterday's close minus today's close.

Table 5.6 gives us two key results that will ultimately be used to define RSI. The relative momentum over four days

Table 5.5 Relative and Absolute Momentum

Date	S&P-500	Relative Momentum	Absolute Momentum
11/29/91	375.22		
12/02/91	381.40	6.18	6.18
12/03/91	380.96	−0.44	0.44
12/04/91	380.07	−0.89	0.89
12/05/91	377.39	−2.68	2.68
Total	2.17	2.17	10.19

Relative momentum = close of today − close of yesterday.
Absolute momentum = |close of today − close of yesterday|.
4-day momentum = $377.39 - 375.22 = 2.17$.

Table 5.6 Momentum Separated for Up and Down Days

Date	S&P-500	Relative Momentum	Absolute Momentum	Up-Day Momentum	Down-Day Momentum
11/29/91	375.22				
12/02/92	381.40	6.18	6.18	6.18	0.00
12/03/91	380.96	−0.44	0.44	0.00	0.44
12/04/91	380.07	−0.89	0.89	0.00	0.89
12/05/91	377.39	−2.68	2.68	0.00	2.68
Total	377.39− 375.22= 2.17	2.17	10.19	6.18 (S_u)	4.01 (S_d)

is the difference between the up day momentum and down day momentum over four days (2.17 = 6.18 − 4.01). Also, the absolute momentum is the sum of the up-day momentum and down-day momentum (10.19 = 6.18 + 4.01). Let S_u and S_d be the sum of the up-day and down-day momentum over a given number of days. We can summarize these results in the following equations:

$$\begin{aligned} \text{momentum} &= S_u - S_d, \\ |\text{momentum}| &= S_u + S_d. \end{aligned} \qquad (5.12)$$

We can solve these two equations for S_u using algebra. Simply add the two equations and gather terms to find:

$$S_u = 0.5 * (\text{momentum} + |\text{momentum}|). \qquad (5.13)$$

You can verify this result from the data in Table 5.6 (S_u = 0.5 * (10.19 + 2.17) = 6.18). We will use these results to define Wilder's RSI (see Bibliography).

Calculating RSI

The relative strength index measures the proportion of momentum change over a given period caused by momentum on up days. This will become clear from the following definition:

$$RSI = 100 * (RS/(1 + RS)). \qquad (5.14)$$

Here, RS is the ratio of average momentum over the last n days on up days versus down days. The revised equation looks like this:

$$RS = A_u/A_d. \qquad (5.15)$$

Since the number of days in both averages is the same, we can multiply both averages by the number of days in the average. This converts the averages into the sum of the momentum on up days and down days. Hence, we can rewrite RS in terms of S_u and S_d, as shown below:

$$RS = S_u/S_d. \tag{5.16}$$

We can now rewrite the RSI definition using the new RS definition. This gives us an RSI definition in terms of the sum of the momentum on up days and down days.

$$RSI = 100*(S_u)/(S_u + S_d) \tag{5.17}$$

We can continue our process of adjustment to reflect the relationship between relative momentum, absolute momentum, S_u and S_d. For instance, we can rewrite RSI using absolute momentum and relative momentum:

$$RSI = 100*(0.5*(\text{momentum} + |\text{momentum}|))/(|\text{momentum}|),$$
$$= 50*(\text{momentum} + |\text{momentum}|)/(|\text{momentum}|). \tag{5.18}$$

We have found an important result here that directly ties RSI into relative and absolute momentum. Over x days, the RSI is the proportion of absolute momentum because of up days. Hence, the x-day RSI is equivalent to the x-day momentum.

In Table 5.7, we did the RSI calculations using the sum of up-day and down-day momentum. Next, we will redo the 4-day RSI calculations using the relative and absolute momentum to show that we get the same value using either method (see Table 5.8). Now it is easier to understand what the RSI is trying to capture by using the ideas of relative and absolute momentum.

Rather than use Wilder's original method, we like to use

Table 5.7   Calculating 4-Day RSI Using Sum of Up-Day and
Down-Day Momentum

Date	S&P-500	Up-Day Momentum (S_u)	Down-Day Momentum (S_d)	RSI
11/29/91	375.22			
12/02/92	381.40	6.18	0.00	
12/03/91	380.96	0.00	0.44	
12/04/91	380.07	0.00	0.89	
12/05/91	377.39	0.00	2.68	
Total		6.18	4.01	60.65

RSI = 100*(6.18)/(6.18+4.01) = 60.64769382.

Table 5.8   Calculating 4-Day RSI Using Relative and
Absolute Momentum

Date	S&P-500	Relative Momentum	Absolute Momentum	RSI
11/29/91	375.22			
12/02/92	381.40	6.18	6.18	
12/03/91	380.96	−0.44	0.44	
12/04/91	380.07	−0.89	0.89	
12/05/91	377.39	−2.68	2.68	
Total		2.17	10.19	60.65

RSI = 50*(2.17+10.19)/(10.19) = 60.64769382.

all available data to calculate RSI and then smooth it with a
simple moving average. Wilder's method effectively uses a
27-day exponential moving average to smooth daily S_u and
S_d values before computing RSI, but this smoothing often
masks the underlying price extremes. It also makes the RSI
take on the appearance of the price curve.

STOCHASTIC RSI OSCILLATOR

As an RSI user, you may have been frustrated when the RSI did not reach an extreme value (above 80 or below 20) for months at a time. Perhaps you wanted an entry point into an ongoing trend, and were looking for a price extreme, but couldn't find one using RSI. The solution to your problem is the Stochastic RSI (StochRSI), which we will now discuss as the second element in our package of momentum oscillators.

The stochastic RSI oscillator combines the two popular ideas behind the RSI and the stochastic oscillator. The stochastic oscillator measures the location of closing prices within the recent high to low range. Similarly, StochRSI measures the location of RSI within its recent range, showing short-term momentum extremes. It can be used as an anti-trend or a trend-following tool.

The sensitivity of the StochRSI overcomes the disadvantages of using a fixed number of days in its calculation and the tendency of the built-in RSI smoothing to mask short-lived price extremes while showing swing failures in RSI. The ability to spot short-term extremes in RSI (and momentum) is its principal advantage. The stochastic RSI is a more consistent indicator of overbought and oversold conditions simply because we are measuring its position within the most recent range. The stochRSI is defined as follows:

$$\text{stochRSI} = (\text{RSI} - \text{RSI}_L)/(\text{RSI}_H - \text{RSI}_L). \qquad (5.19)$$

Here RSI_H and RSI_L are the highest and lowest values of RSI over a given look-back period. Whenever RSI makes a new low, the stochRSI will be at 0. This is an example of a failure swing in a down move. During an upmove, the RSI will make new highs (over the calculation period) and the stochRSI will be near 1.0. Thus, you could use stochRSI both as an overbought/oversold oscillator and to follow trends in RSI. Divergences are also evident on the stochRSI plots, which means you can combine all the different elements of RSI analysis into the single stochRSI indicator.

For symmetry, we use the same number of days in the look-back period as those in the RSI calculations, but you can experiment with different calculation periods if you wish. For example, if we calculate a 14-period RSI, then we will find RSI_H and RSI_L over 14 periods. The values of stochRSI vary between $+1$ and 0. When RSI is at its highest value, stochRSI has a value of $+1$. Conversely, when RSI is at its lowest value, stochRSI is at 0. You can multiply stochRSI by 100 if you wish. Again, remember that you have some smoothing built in to the RSI numbers that varies with the software package.

Case in Point: StochRSI, RSI, and the T-Bond Market

Figure 5.19 shows the September, 1993 T-Bond contract, a 14-day RSI, and a 14-day stochRSI. The SuperCharts graphics package plots lines at RSI values of 80 and 20 for overbought and oversold conditions. During the nine and a half months of trading shown, the RSI never reached an oversold or over-bought condition. It did come close to becoming over-bought a few times. Note that the RSI pattern is similar to the pattern of closing prices, with one notable divergence at the highs in March, 1993: Price made a new high, while RSI was virtually flat. Other than that, RSI moved in sync with prices.

In the same figure, the 14-day stochRSI showed short-term and intermediate-term market extremes far better than the RSI. A stochRSI value of 0 provided excellent entry points into the uptrend. The divergence between stochRSI and prices is noteworthy at the peaks in March. During strong, brief uptrends, stochRSI remained pinned at 1.0, showing the strength of the move. Note the sell signal in April when stochRSI first fell away from its highs. Note also the buy signals in January, February, and April, as the T-Bond market

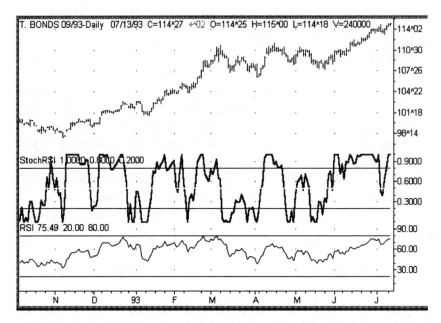

FIGURE 5.19 A comparison of the 14-day RSI to the 14-day stochRSI for the T-Bond 09/93 contract.

corrected or consolidated. These signals are unmistakably evident in the stochRSI plot, but not as obviously evident in the RSI plot. Thus, the stochRSI analysis is more useful in this example.

In Figure 5.20 we show a close-up of the T-Bond September 1993 contract from February through June, 1993. The stochRSI showed each significant overbought and oversold condition over this period, flagging a short-term tradeable move. The divergence in March that we spotted in Figure 5.19 can be seen on an expanded scale here. Buying around the 0.2 level and selling around the 0.8 level would have been profitable. It's important to reenter the market if stochRSI again rises above 0.80 or falls below 0.20. Say you sold the bonds when the stochRSI fell below 0.80 in early June; the uptrend resumed and the stochRSI again moved above 0.80

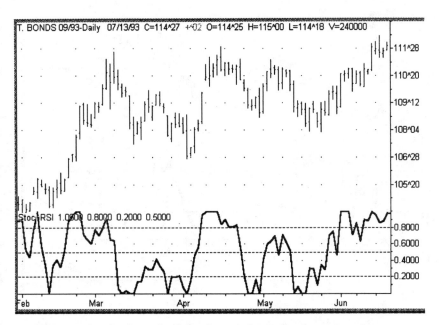

T. BONDS 09/93-Daily 07/13/93 C=114^27 +^02 O=114^25 H=115^00 L=114^18 V=240000

FIGURE 5.20   A closer look at the stochRSI for the T-Bond contract.

towards 1.0. It would have been best to reverse the short position to a long trade in keeping with the stochRSI moving above 0.80.

Case in Point: StochRSI and S&P-500 Index

Figure 5.21 shows the action of the S&P-500 index for approximately seven months from October, 1992 through April, 1993. The market was trending up to mid-December, and then entered a broad trading range. The 14-period RSI did not exceed 80 nor fall below 20 throughout this period. Thus, it could not be used as an overbought/oversold indicator.

The stochRSI showed each major price extreme, though it showed choppy action during some periods of the trading range. A sell signal occurred when the stochRSI was above

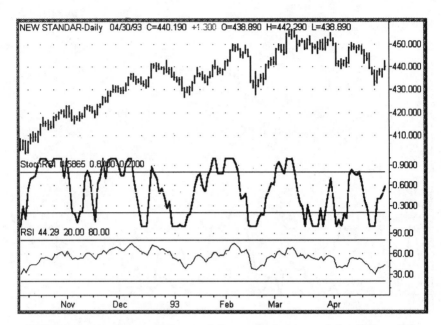

FIGURE 5.21 A comparison of the performance of the RSI and the stochRSI over a time interval in which the S&P-500 index moved up and entered a broad trading range.

0.80 and then fell below that level. A buy signal occurred when this indicator was below 0.20 and then exceeded that level. Note the reversal condition: If the stochRSI reverses after crossing above 0.20 or rises after falling below 0.80, then you should reverse the buy or sell signal. The reversal condition occurs because stochRSI can stay above 0.80 during uptrends and below 0.20 during downtrends for the duration of the trend.

Next, we'll look at the S&P-500 index in Figure 5.22 covering the period November, 1991 through February, 1992. Note how the 14-day stochRSI in this figure weakened all through December, 1991 as the index moved up to the 330 area and then entered a tight trading range. The stochRSI settled at 0 showing a downtrend just before the decline to

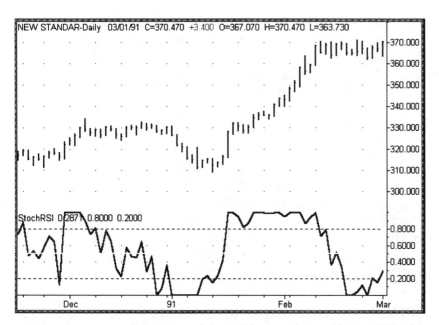

FIGURE 5.22   An illustration of the stochRSI indicator during a trending period in the S&P-500 index.

the 310 area, and it moved off its bottom two days before the index itself bottomed. The index and stochRSI rose strongly in January until the stochRSI was at 1.00, indicating a strong uptrend. The stochRSI remained above 0.80 for the entire rise into February, again falling off within a day of the high for the move. As the index entered a trading range, the stochRSI fell off again dropping to 0.

The important idea to grasp here is that the stochRSI fell when the index entered a trading range. The stochRSI is quick to react at both bottoms and tops, so you can trade it only when it is at an extreme, showing a trend. Accordingly, you can buy when it rises above 0.80 and sell when it falls below 0.20. You can then close your position (or reverse) when the values fall below 0.80 or rise above 0.20. Or, you can trade only when the stochRSI falls below 0.50 or rises above 0.50.

You also can use some smoothing to reduce whipsaws, or require stochRSI to close above or below 0.50 for three days before putting on positions. This might delay entry, but it may also reduce whipsaws. In this way, you can adapt this indicator to your trading style.

Trading Strategies with StochRSI

The versatility of the stochRSI can be further illustrated with weekly data for Amgen (AMGN). Figure 5.23 shows a 7-week stochRSI and a 7-week RSI below recent prices. The stochRSI again picked off significant highs and lows that the RSI did not. Note how the fall in stochRSI values was timely indication of the high in Amgen; the stochRSI fell below 0.20

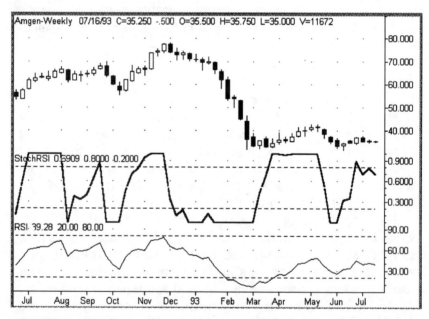

FIGURE 5.23 The stochRSI is shown over a longer time period using weekly data for Amgen.

well before the huge sell off. It also picked most of the small rally that followed. This example also proves the timeliness and sensitivity of stochRSI. You could experiment with different time periods of calculations and action levels, and hence use stochRSI for long- as well as short-term analysis.

But what about using stochRSI to analyze a very short time frame? Figure 5.24 illustrates the use of the stochRSI with hourly data using the September, 1993 T-Bond contract. Here we smoothed the stochRSI heavily to remove the noise inherent in using such a short time frame for analysis. We computed a 20-period RSI and a 20-period stochastic oscillator. Then, we smoothed the 20-period stochastic with a 10-period simple moving average and plotted the slow stochRSI over the hourly price bars shown in this figure.

The momentum rose as prices rose and fell when prices entered a trading range. You can see that the stochRSI can fall even when the market is moving sideways. A sideways

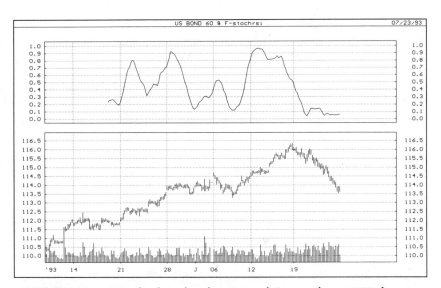

FIGURE 5.24 Hourly data for the T-Bond September, 1993 futures contract is used to illustrate the action of the stochRSI.

move causes a loss of upward momentum that produces lower stochRSI values. Dips in the stochRSI correlate well with lows in the hourly chart. Note the steep decline in stochRSI and how it flattened out at low values (below 0.2) during the market decline.

You could have covered your long when the stochRSI fell below 0.50 at the 116-0 level, and you had a second chance to cover at the 116-0 level when a rebound to that level kept the stochRSI below 0.2. Or, you could have used the bounce to go short near the 116-0 level. When using the stochRSI with hourly data, you should use other indicators to confirm your analysis. For example, you could use a daily bar chart with a short-term moving average to set the trend.

To show RSI's performance in analyzing hourly data, we plotted a 20-period RSI for the hourly US 09/93 T-Bond contract in Figure 5.25. We superimposed a 10-period simple

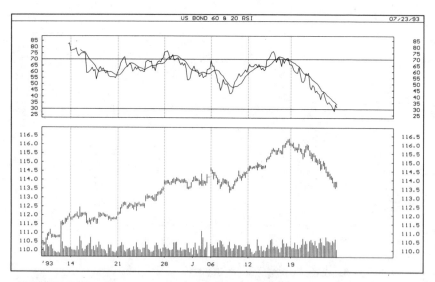

FIGURE 5.25 The 20-period RSI for the hourly T-Bond September, 1993 contract.

moving average on the RSI numbers. The 20-period RSI peaked before the actual high, producing a classic divergence between momentum and prices as they rose to a new high. The RSI declined slowly as prices fell over the next three days. The stochRSI also peaked before prices, and showed the classic divergence as prices made new highs. However, it declined faster than the RSI itself.

You can directly compare the 20-period RSI (solid line) to the smoothed 20-period stochRSI (dotted line) in Figure 5.26. Note how the stochRSI moves faster than the RSI. This makes it valuable for signalling trend changes. For example, the stochRSI fell below its halfway point of 0.50 while the RSI was still near 65. The stochRSI also peaked before the RSI did. It is a more sensitive measure of momentum changes than the RSI.

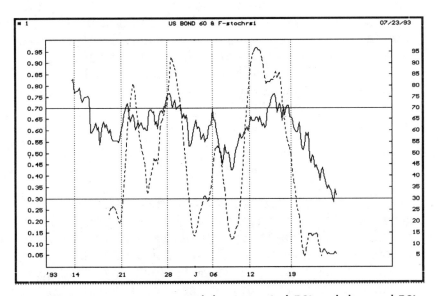

FIGURE 5.26 A comparison of the 20-period RSI and the stochRSI (dotted line) for the hourly September, 1993 T-Bond contract.

VARIABLE LENGTH DYNAMIC MOMENTUM INDEX

The third indicator in our package of momentum oscillators is a variable length RSI, which we'll show you how to build. You'll get the most out of this section if you have software with a "callable" RSI function, that is, a built-in function for RSI with the number of days as its input. The dynamic momentum index (DMI) is specifically designed to use a changing number of days in its calculations; in fact, its length can give you valuable insight into market action. The variable length idea overcomes the effects of smoothing to some degree since smoothing often obscures short-lived market extremes.

In DMI calculations, you use a longer period as volatility decreases, giving a longer range view when the markets are trading quietly. Then, you use fewer periods of data when volatility increases, shortening the horizon for finding overbought or oversold regions in active markets. The variable length distinguishes DMI from CMO and stochRSI. Freed from the constraint of a fixed number of days, DMI gives you insight into the dynamics of market behavior, as prices speed up or slow down. In that sense, extremes in DMI are more likely to provide successful entries for antitrend trades than either CMO or stochRSI.

Indexing DMI to Volatility

One approach for indexing DMI to market volatility is to first calculate the 5-day standard deviation of closing prices. Then, we take a 10-day moving average of the standard deviations. We pick the number of days in the equivalent static RSI; in this case, 14 days. Next, we define the following equations to calculate the number of days in the variable length DMI:

$$Std_A = Average_{10}(Std(C,5)),$$
$$V_i = Std(C,5)/Std_A, \qquad\qquad (5.20)$$
$$T_D = INT(14/V_i).$$

The Std_A is a 10-day simple moving average of the 5-day standard deviation of the close. The volatility index V_i is the ratio of today's value of the 5-day standard deviation divided by its average value over the past 10 days. V_i increases with rising volatility. The T_D divides 14 by the volatility index. The notation INT ensures that we use integer values for the number of days in DMI calculations.

If the index is greater than 1, then T_D is less than 14. Thus, rising volatility reduces the length of the DMI. If the index is less than 1, then T_D increases. We also define lower and upper bounds for the number of days in the calculations.

$$(T_D)_{MAX} = 30 \qquad\qquad (5.21)$$
$$(T_D)_{MIN} = 5$$

We arbitrarily restricted the maximum and minimum number of days used for DMI calculations to 30 and 5. These limits fit our trading horizon, but you can use other limits as you wish.

Be aware that the conversion is nonlinear, arising from the definition of the volatility index itself. The values of the percentage change in V_i will give you a sense of the nonlinearity. The conversion is more sensitive when the index is less than 1 and less sensitive to changes when the index is greater than 2.

As shown, we built the variable length DMI around the static RSI length of 14 days. Hence, when the V_i is approximately 1, the DMI and RSI will have similar values. As the index drops below 1, DMI and RSI values will diverge quickly. As the index increases above 1, DMI and RSI values will diverge slowly. Hence, the exact nature of the DMI-RSI curves will depend on the volatility in the data over the given test period. The divergence will increase as volatility increases.

Case in Point: DMI and Dow Jones Industrial Average

Figure 5.27 shows a direct comparison of a 14-period RSI and DMI for the Dow Jones Industrial Average (DJIA). The DMI leads RSI into overbought and oversold regions.

We'll use DJIA data from the trading range in early 1991 to show how the length of DMI varies. Figure 5.28 shows the scaled length of DMI plotted below the DJIA daily close. We multiplied the days in the DMI by 10 and added to 2550 to give the scaled values. You can now directly compare the length of DMI with market action.

Every period of market volatility reduced the length of DMI. When the market traded quietly, the length of DMI increased. Note the short length used for DMI calculations

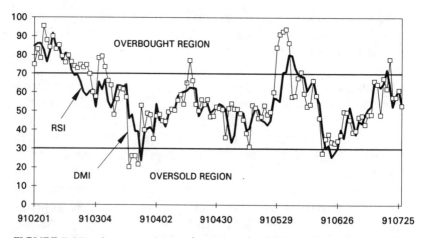

FIGURE 5.27 A comparison of unsmoothed RSI and the DMI for the Dow Jones Industrial Average data.

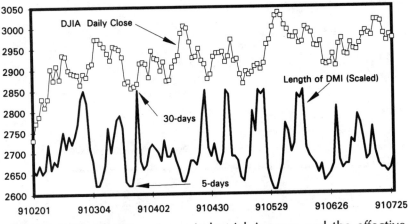

FIGURE 5.28   The Dow Jones Industrial Average and the effective length of the DMI.

in early March, late March, mid-April, late May, and mid-June. In each instance, the market was making quick moves.

This example makes it clear that you can use the DMI to identify overbought or oversold conditions. DMI usually leads RSI into the extreme regions by one or more days (see Figure 5.27), and this lead time can prove valuable to many you. Because DMI length is more closely tied to market dynamics, the extremes that DMI shows are more likely to lead to profitable antitrend trades than the extremes shown by stochRSI. In other words, DMI is more selective about showing extremes. You can also use DMI to develop flexible parameter trading models.

Case in Point: DMI and the S&P-500 Index

Figure 5.29 compares a 14-day RSI to a 14-day DMI for the S&P-500 index. You can see that the RSI was more or less flat over the test period, moving in a narrow range. The DMI,

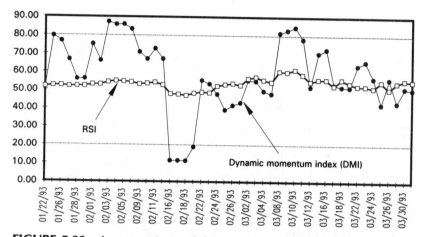

FIGURE 5.29 A comparison of the 14-day RSI and the 14-day DMI for the S&P-500 index data in Figure 5.30.

on the other hand, showed overbought and oversold conditions on four occasions over this period.

In Figure 5.30, we overlaid the DMI on the S&P-500 index daily close. You can see that the extremes in DMI correspond to extremes in the index as well. One trading strategy is to buy when the DMI goes below 20 and then rises up. You would sell when the DMI is above 80 and then crosses below this level. This approach would have given tradeable signals three times in February-March, 1993. Each signal preceded substantial moves by about two days. This provides you with is a significant edge in trading.

Finally, Figure 5.31 shows the effective length, that is, number of days, used for these DMI calculations. Low values correspond to periods of high volatility. Conversely, high values for the effective length imply periods of low volatility. You can see from Figure 5.30 that quick moves in the market reduced the effective length of DMI calculations.

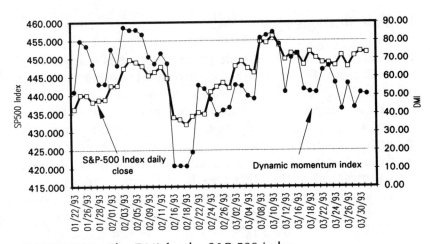

FIGURE 5.30 The DMI for the S&P-500 index.

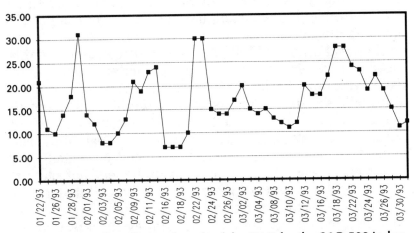

FIGURE 5.31 The effective length of the DMI for the S&P-500 index.

Trading Strategies with DMI

There are a myriad of possible trading strategies that you can use with DMI. In this section, we give brief summaries of the situations that lend themselves to trading with DMI.

Let's say trendiness indicators such as r^2 and absCMO do not show any trends, implying that an antitrend strategy has the greater chance of success. You would use an overbought condition to go short and an oversold condition to go long. For example, when the DMI signals an overbought condition today, you could go short tomorrow a bit below the low of today. The reverse is true for a long position. You could use a tight stop above the highest high of the last five days for short trades. For long trades you could place a stop below the lowest low of the last 5 days.

In contrast, if the market is trending, as measured by the ADX or linear regression, you could use DMI as the entry point for trades in the direction of the trend. For example, if the market were trending higher, you would wait for an oversold signal from the DMI. You would then assume that this was a minor correction within an uptrend and, thus, a low risk-buying opportunity. The opposite is true in a downtrend. You would sell after an overbought condition within a downtrend. For example, you could sell below the lowest low of the last three days with a stop at the highest high of the last three days. A cautionary note: You should adequately test both strategies and be comfortable with the odds of success.

In a market trending higher or lower, many traders use DMI as an exit tool by exiting on an overbought condition. Note that the market does not have to reverse direction automatically simply because it is overbought or oversold. An extreme price condition often shows that the market has high momentum in that direction. Thus, an overbought market could go higher and an oversold market could go lower.

Finally, remember that the main advantage of using DMI is that you do not have to specify the number of days in the calculations. DMI will adjust the number of days based on market volatility. The construction of your volatility index determines the sensitivity of DMI.

SUMMARY

Our new momentum oscillators make up a group of powerful tools to analyze momentum. The Chande momentum oscillator (CMO) is a pure momentum oscillator that shows net momentum change on a bounded scale. Its critical difference from the RSI is that it does not use built-in smoothing in its calculations. The CMO can be used to find market extremes, often showing extremes that the RSI does not. It can also be used to trade momentum changes using the zero-crossing of the indicator.

You can combine CMO values from different time intervals to find a composite CMO. The combination can be created by simple averaging or weighted by volatility. This volatility-based composite CMO offers a sensitive view of multi-interval momentum changes. You can also filter the CMO to reduce noise in the data and locate truly significant price extremes. Thus, the CMO is a powerful and flexible momentum oscillator.

The stochastic RSI indicates where the current RSI values lies within its recent range. It can be used both as an overbought or oversold indicator, as well as an indicator of failure swings in the RSI. It can, therefore, combine the two approaches to analysis of momentum using RSI. In particular, it is an excellent short-term oscillator, often showing extremes that RSI does not.

Lastly, the Dynamic Momentum Index lets us calculate RSI without specifying the number of days in the calculations. It adjusts its length based on market volatility. This helps overcome a key limitation of RSI. The DMI often leads RSI into overbought or oversold regions by several days. Such early warnings could prove extremely useful to you.

6
Market Thrust and Thrust Oscillator

This chapter introduces powerful new indicators that combine items of data unique to the stock market and unavailable for the futures markets. These four data items are the number of advancing (AI) and declining issues (DI) and advancing (AV) and declining volume (DV). The AI and DI count issues without regard to the extent of price change or the market capitalization.

Market analysts usually look at these data in a variety of ways. On days when the market is up strongly, AI > DI by more than 1000, and AV > DV by a factor of 3:1 or more. Thus, the advancing volume could easily be four times (or more) than the declining volume. Similarly, there is general agreement that, on days when the market is very weak, AI < DI by several hundred issues, and DV > AV by a ratio of 3:1 or more.

On days when the markets move decisively in either direction, we see a pattern in which AI > DI, AV > DV or AI < DI, AV < DV. There also can be other combinations of these variables, which produce ambiguous cases because it's common to analyze the advancing and declining issues as one block, and the up and down volume as another block. These blocks, then, do not always move together because of the randomness in trading.

The popular Arms index devised by Richard Arms combines the two blocks of data into a single indicator. He devised this trader's index, (commonly called TRIN) to show when abnormally high volume was going into advancing or declining stocks. It is defined as

$$\text{Arms Index} = \frac{(AI/DI)}{(AV/DV)} = \frac{(DV/DI)}{(AV/AI)} \tag{6.1}$$

where $AI = \#$ Advancing issues, $AV =$ Advancing Volume, $DI = \#$ Declining issues and $DV =$ Declining volume.

The Arms Index is the ratio of the average volume in declining issues to the average volume in advancing issues; it measures relative volume flows. A reading of 1.00 is neutral; a value greater than 1.0 indicates more volume in declining issues, while a value below 1.0 shows more advancing volume. The direction and speed of the changing index values is often more important than the absolute value of the index itself.

On a day when the market is weak, the Arms index is greater than 1.0 since there is more volume in declining issues. When the market is up strongly, the index is less than 1.0. Note that the scales for up days and down days are not the same. This occurs because the Arms index is bounded between 0 and 1 for up days, but unbounded beyond 1 on weak days. For example, readings greater than 4.0 have been recorded many times. This makes it difficult to use TRIN with moving averages. We'll rearrange the terms in the Arm's Index one more time to clarify this idea:

$$\text{Arms Index} = \frac{(AI/DI)}{(AV/DV)} = \frac{(AI * DV)}{(DI * AV)} \tag{6.2}$$

Because the index multiplies AI by DV, and DI by AV, it can produce unusual effects in "mixed" markets, that is, when AI > DI but AV < DV, or AI < DI but AV > DV. It is intuitively contradictory to have the index driven by the product of AI*DV (and DI*AV) rather than AI*AV (and DI*DV). When we have "one-sided" markets, we expect greater volume, or more stocks, or both moving in that direction (up or down).

The primary application of TRIN is to detect overbought or oversold conditions in the market. Since the daily data tend to be noisy and apparently trendless, the daily TRIN is usually smoothed with a 10-day simple moving average (SMA) to isolate the underlying trend. When the 10-day SMA of TRIN rises above 1.20, the market is thought to be oversold. The market is thought to be overbought if the 10-day SMA of the TRIN falls below 0.80. The market is expected to trend higher after an oversold TRIN condition, and trend lower after an overbought TRIN reading. The 10-day SMA is considered an intermediate-term indicator.

There are three difficulties with using TRIN:

1. The ratios used in TRIN often obscure market action. This is particularly true when we have "mixed" market action.
2. The very process of smoothing TRIN with moving averages distorts the picture of relative volume flows.
3. The TRIN has a bounded scale for up-side activity, but an unbounded scale for down-side activity.

We developed our market thrust indicators to overcome these weaknesses. You'll see these features more clearly in the following discussion on market thrust and the thrust oscillator.

MARKET THRUST AND THRUST OSCILLATOR

A more consistent approach to analyzing AI, DI, AV, and DV data is to look at the product of the number of shares advancing or declining and the volume going into those shares, that is, using the products AI*AV and DI*DV. The thrust, or power of the move, is measured by the number of stocks and the volume going into those stocks.

For example, if 5 stocks advanced on 100 shares, the thrust is 500; next, if 7 stocks advanced on 90 shares, the thrust is 630. Thus, we would say there was greater market thrust the second day. This definition is intuitively more satisfying because "one-sided" action means greater volume, or more stocks, or both, moving in that direction. If we had used average volume, on the first day it was $100/5 = 20$ versus $90/7 = 13$. Using ratios, as in TRIN, we would say there was more activity on the first day. This small example illustrates the difference between TRIN and market thrust (MT). We define the market thrust MT as:

$$MT = (AI*AV - DI*DV)/1{,}000{,}000. \qquad (6.3)$$

We divide the thrust by 1,000,000 to give reasonably small numbers for convenience and simplicity. You do not have to divide by 1,000,000 at all; you could choose any other scaling constant. The daily number may be used to spot large moves in one direction. The thrust is cumulated to identify underlying trends, and these can be smoothed or summed for trading purposes. Thus, you can have a cumulative MT-line, which is a volumetric advance-decline line:

$$MT\text{-line}_{today} = MT + MT\text{-line}_{yesterday} \qquad (6.4)$$

We can define a thrust oscillator (TO) to compare relative volume flows:

$$TO = \frac{(AI*AV - DI*DV)}{(AI*AV + DI*DV)} * 100 \qquad (6.5)$$

The multiplication by 100 is optional, so that TO varies between +1 and −1 or +100 and −100. There is important difference between MT and TO: TO values are always between +1 and −1 (or +100 and −100) but MT values are unbounded.

The thrust oscillator definition has many advantages. The biggest advantage is that it has the same scale for up and down days. The range of values is bounded between the same numbers on either side. This is in contrast to TRIN, which is bounded for up days but unbounded for down days.

The second advantage of TO, is that it depicts upthrust (AI*AV) and downdraft (DI*DV), so that a strong up day or strong down day is identified consistently. TRIN, as shown in Table 6.1, sometimes obscures a strong one-sided up or down action. A third advantage of TO over TRIN is that it shows the net balance between bullish and bearish activity on a given day. Lastly, it presents consistent information; TO

TABLE 6.1 Simulated market data comparing TRIN, MT and TO

Day	AI	AV	DI	DV	TRIN	MT	TO
1	1000	1,000,000	100	100,000	1.0	990	0.98
2	100	100,000	1000	1,000,000	1.0	−990	−0.98
3	1000	1,000,000	100	200,000	2.0	980	0.96
4	100	200,000	1000	1,000,000	0.50	−980	−0.96
5	800	800,000	400	400,000	1.0	480	0.60
6	600	600,000	600	600,000	1.0	0	0.0
7	800	700,000	400	500,000	1.40	360	0.47
8	800	900,000	400	300,000	0.67	600	0.71
9	600	700,000	600	500,000	0.71	120	0.17
10	700	600,000	500	600,000	1.40	120	0.17
11	600	500,000	600	700,000	1.40	−120	−0.17
12	700	500,000	500	700,000	1.96	0	0
13	500	600,000	700	600,000	0.71	−120	−0.17
14	500	700,000	700	500,000	0.52	0	0
15	500	400,000	700	800,000	1.43	−360	−0.47
16	400	500,000	800	700,000	0.70	−360	−0.47
17	400	400,000	800	800,000	1.00	−480	−0.60

provides normalized volume flows and can be used as an overbought/oversold indicator.

Variations of MT and TO

Consider the special case when there are unit volume flows into advancing and declining issues, where AV=DV = 1. In this case, the AV (or DV) term merely acts as a constant multiplier, and the MT-line simply collapses to the usual cumulative Advance-Decline (A-D) line, since:

$$MT = (AI - DI) \ (AV=DV = 1),$$
$$MT\text{-line}_{today} = (AI - DI) + MT\text{-line}_{yesterday}. \tag{6.6}$$

Therefore, we can expect a broad similarity between the cumulative MT-line and the A-D line. The two often diverge at turning points when volume rotates predominantly into advancing or declining issues. Therefore, the MT-line is more useful an the A-D line at turning points.

Next, consider the special case when AV=DV, which converts the TO into a variant of the advance-decline ratio since:

$$TO = (AI-DI)/(AI+DI) \ \ (if \ AV=DV). \tag{6.7}$$

If AV=DV, then TO becomes the net advancing or declining stocks as a fraction of total stocks traded. TO may also be considered a variant of a volume oscillator because if AI=DI, then:

$$TO = (AV-DV)/(AV+DV) \ \ (if \ AI=DI). \tag{6.8}$$

This makes TO an effective net volume oscillator; it works as a combination of an issues oscillator and a volume oscillator at the same time. A plot of TO looks similar to a volume oscillator plot or an issues oscillator plot, which is an unusual but useful feature.

Our market thrust idea captures most of the variations missed by TRIN. The product of AI*AV and DI*DV shows the amount of up or down thrust. We can sort out the different combinations of AI, DI and AV, DV more accurately by using market thrust than with TRIN. We'll compare and contrast TO and TRIN in the next section.

Case in Point: Comparing MT, TO, and TRIN

We developed fictitious data to illustrate each of the different combinations of AI, DI, AV, and DV that could occur in actual trading. The fictitious data merely facilitate our discussion of different market conditions using similar numbers for each occurrence. Later, we'll use real data to make our case.

In Table 6.1, day 1 is strong up and day 2 is strong down; however, TRIN shows they are neutral. In contrast, MT shows the exceptional strength and weakness of each day, and TO is at positive and negative extremes each day. Remember that the unbounded MT could exceed the +990 or −990 values recorded here, but TO will remain between +1 and −1.

Day 3 is also a strong up day, but has somewhat greater down volume than day 1. TRIN flags it as a bearish day since the average volume in declining stocks is greater than the average volume in advancing stocks. The volume disparity occurred even though advances led declines by 900 stocks. Note, however, that the thrust value of 980 shows day 3 was almost as strong as day 1. Thus, MT was more consistent with its values on days 1 through 3 than TRIN.

Day 4 is a reversal of day 3, with 900 more declines and volume predominantly in declining shares. Hence, it was a bearish day. Nevertheless, TRIN calls this an overbought day with bullish demand, because average volume in advancing shares was greater. Note how Thrust reads -980, and TO - 0.96, capturing the bearish mood of the day. Day 5 is neutral says TRIN; MT says it is moderately strong on the upside. This shows that TRIN does not consistently show bearish or bullish market activity.

TRIN correctly calls day 8 a bullish day, as do MT and TO, but calls day 9 more bullish than day 8. Thrust correctly calls day 9 mildly bullish, because up volume exceeded down volume. Here an equal number of stocks advanced and declined. TRIN is bearish on day 10, while Thrust is unchanged from day 9, correctly calling the mildly bullish day.

Day 11 provides a striking contrast between TRIN and MT and TO. TRIN calls it strongly bearish; MT and TO call it a standoff. It is the same story for day 14: TRIN says great bullish demand, Thrust is dead neutral. Here the divergent internal dynamics of TRIN give conflicting values.

Relative volume flows, defined as DI/DV and AI/AV, simply do not consistently show if the market action was evenly split or one-sided among the four variables. In contrast, because of their definitions, both MT and TO clearly show when the action was evenly split or one-sided among these variables, and provide a more consistent picture of market action than TRIN.

In essence, using the product of AI*AV and DI*DV eliminates the confusion that results from taking the DV/DI and AV/AI ratios found in TRIN. What's more, we can easily use moving averages to smooth MT and TO in order to reduce noise and see the underlying changes more accurately.

Case in Point: Thrust Oscillator and the Crash of 1987

Now we'll look at real market data using the thrust oscillator. TO is bounded between +1 and −1 (or +100 and −100), having the same scale for up and down days. Conversely, TRIN is unbounded on down days.

Figure 6.1 shows the Dow Jones Industrial Average (DJIA) from June, 1987 through November, 1988 and a 10-day SMA of TRIN. This period covers a new record high and the market collapse of October, 1987, including the sideways action that followed. The values of smoothed TRIN rose to nearly 2.50 during the collapse. It is difficult to see any other notable overbought or oversold conditions using TRIN.

Figure 6.2 shows the same market period and a plot of the 21 day SMA of TO. You can see immediately that TO dropped to just under −0.30 in October, 1987. The previous peak in TO occurred above 0.30 in June, followed by successively lower peaks in August (at the top) and early October. This was clear evidence that the market was losing its upward thrust as it surged to new highs in August and tried a weak rally in late September. The market again reached overbought readings in January, 1988 and March, 1988, followed by small corrections.

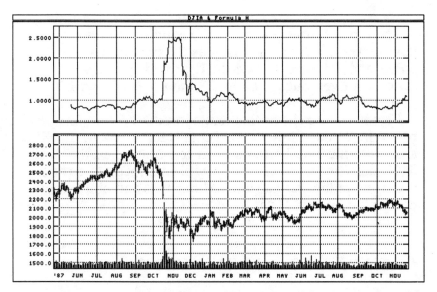

FIGURE 6.1   A 10-day simple moving average of the Arms index and the Dow Jones Industrial Average in 1987–88.

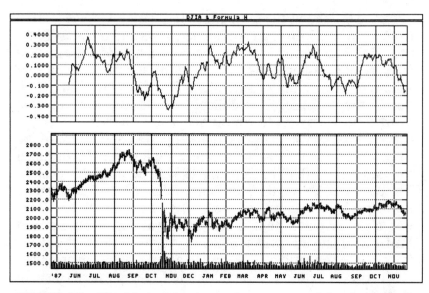

FIGURE 6.2   The 21-day simple moving average of the thrust oscillator for the same period as in Figure 6.1.

These two figures show that TO handled the huge volume flows of the crash just as easily as the quiet period that preceded and followed the crash. It provided consistent indications of overbought (0.2 to 0.3) and oversold areas (−0.2 to 0.3).

Figure 6.2 also shows that long-term market bottoms occur when the 21-day SMA of the TO falls to, or below, the −0.3 area. Intermediate bottoms seem to occur when the 21-day SMA falls to the −0.20 area, with intermediate term tops occurring in the 0.2-0.30 area. Minor tops and bottoms often occur with 21-day TO at 0.1 or −0.1.

Case in Point: TO and DJIA in 1990–91

The market had another October massacre in 1990 and moved up into a trading range in 1991. Figure 6.3 shows the

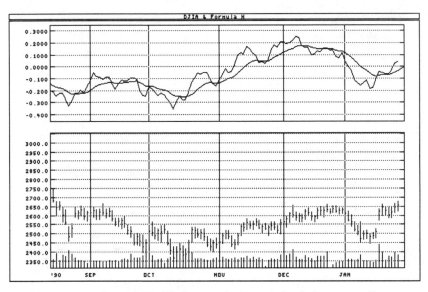

FIGURE 6.3 The DJIA and the 21-day smoothed thrust oscillator at the market bottom in 1990.

market bottom in October-November, 1990 using the 21-day simple moving average of TO and TRIN. Here again, the smoothed TO made two trips below the −0.30 in September and October, 1990. The smoothed TO slipped under its own 13-day exponential average in December, tipping off the brief correction into mid-January. The smoothed TO values were greater than 0.20 during intermediate bottoms.

Figure 6.4 shows the same period with a 21-day smoothed TRIN. It went higher until peaking above 1.2 in October, then fell steadily into late-December. The 21-day smoothed TRIN did not warn of the correction until the end of December. It was more than 10 days slower than the smoothed TO in giving this signal.

In Figure 6.5 you can see the price progress into 1991 off the October, 1990 lows. The market stayed in a trading range for most of the year. Note how the 21-day smoothed TO gave consistent oversold signals near the −0.20 level. The one in

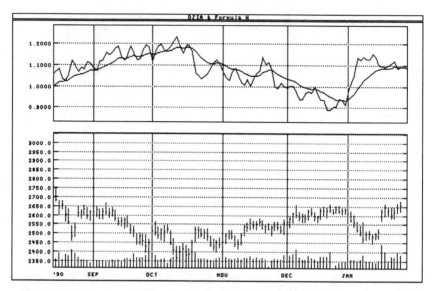

FIGURE 6.4 The 21-day smoothed Arms index for the same period peaked at 1.20 at the market bottom in 1990.

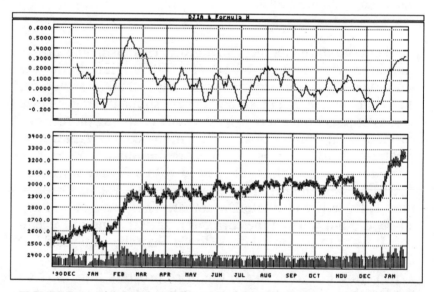

FIGURE 6.5 The DJIA and the 21-day smoothed thrust oscillator with the market in a narrow range.

154

December was particularly timely. Note also the strong market thrust in January–February, 1990 that took the 21-day smoothed TO to the 0.50 area. Such market thrusts often signal higher prices 12 months into the future.

In Figure 6.6, we compare the 21-day smoothed TO (lower curve) to the 21-day smoothed TRIN (upper curve). Notice that TO and TRIN mirror one another. The smoothed TRIN showed oversold conditions near values 1.1; TO and TRIN, however, do not peak at the same values, which is what we expect in a trading range. For example, smoothed TRIN dropped to the 0.70 area in both February and August. However, TO was at 0.50 in February, and only 0.20 in August. Thus, the thrust was much stronger in February than in August.

Similarly, the smoothed TRIN rose above 1.1 on seven occasions, whereas the TO approached its level of −0.20 level

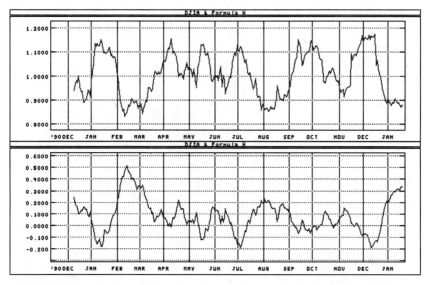

FIGURE 6.6 A comparison of the 21-day smoothed thrust oscillator and Arms index (upper graph) for the 1991 period shown in Figure 6.5.

just three times during the year. For example, the May peak in smoothed TRIN dropped the TO to just the −0.1 level. Finally, the smoothed TRIN stayed flat in early December, but the TO moved up sooner off its bottom.   .

In short, this comparison in trending and flat markets shows that the TO is a better oscillator than TRIN because its signals are more consistent and timely.

Trading Strategies with TO

To see an example of short term trading using TO, look at Figure 6.7. Here you can see a 5-day simple moving average of the TO (upper graph) and the S&P-500 index closes for the first half of 1993. To generate trading signals, we have also superimposed a 5-day exponential moving average

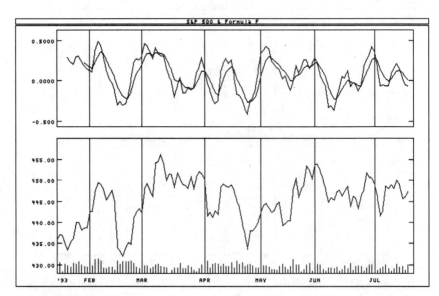

FIGURE 6.7   A 5-day smoothed thrust oscillator for short-term trading combined with its a 5-day exponential moving average.

(EMA) on the 5-day SMA of TO. A buy signal occurs when the 5-day SMA first turns up after a downswing, or crosses above its own 5-day EMA. A sell signal occurs when the SMA crosses under its trailing EMA. These are short-term buy and sell signals because they last only a few days at a time. The plot suggests that such a strategy would have been profitable.

TO can also be useful in providing long-term buy signals. Assuming we could replicate the Dow Jones Industrial Average (through a suitable mutual fund), the gains and losses would be similar to those in Table 6.2 of DJIA signals using TO. These calculations provide a potentially useful long-term indicator. This table shows that there has not been a significant correction in the stock market through mid-1993 after the bottom in August–October, 1990.

To create the long term indicator tested in Table 6.2, we first calculated TO and then plotted a 21-day simple moving average of the TO, adding a second 13-day exponential moving average of this SMA. A buy signal occurs when the 21-day SMA of TO goes below −0.3 then crosses above its own 13-day EMA. We enter the market on the close the next day.

Though TO does a good job of showing long-term bottom, long-term tops are harder to find using an SMA. Market tops seem to occur in response to external factors, and those oc-

Table 6.2 DJIA Buy Signals from TO (Rounded)

Date	Buy	3 MOS%	6 MOS%	12 MOS%	24 MOS%
03-Apr-80	784.00	13.27	21.17	28.44	6.89
28-Sep-81	842.00	3.33	−2.26	9.14	48.81
23-Jun-82	813.00	13.78	28.54	48.71	39.11
24-Feb-84	1165.00	−5.32	6.09	9.61	45.75
05-Nov-87	1985.00	−3.78	1.76	8.06	30.83
08-Feb-90	2644.00	3.37	3.40	7.03	22.73
27-Aug-90	2611.00	−2.60	10.65	15.89	24.63
18-Oct-90	2452.00	7.91	22.31	25.49	30.02
Average		3.74	11.46	19.05	31.10

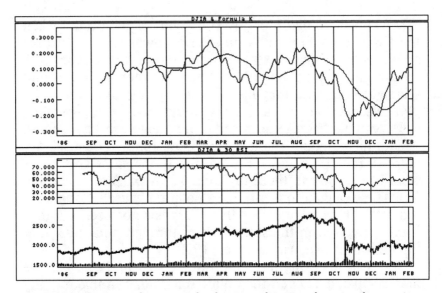

FIGURE 6.8 A 50-day smoothed TO and its 50-day simple moving average (upper graph) at the market top of 1987. The lower graph shows the 30-day RSI and the DJIA.

curring since 1980 did so with an overbought condition followed by a drop in the 50-day smoothed TO below its own 50-day simple moving average. This means that downside thrust increased after the top and led to an intermediate-to-long term bottom with the 30-day TO average dropping to the −0.2 to −0.3 area. In Figure 6.8, you can see the market top in 1987. In particular, note how the market was overbought (30-day RSI over 0.70) and the 50-day smoothed TO (upper graph) fell below its 50-day moving average. This short position began in late August, well before the major selling episodes. The graph also shows that this approach is not perfect and should be used with caution.

SUMMARY

We hope you can see from the previous discussion that market thrust is a powerful new way to analyze stock market action. The thrust oscillator TO provides more consistent readings than TRIN and can be smoothed with averages without distortion. The TO combines an advance/decline oscillator with a volume oscillator to provide a uniquely sensitive market indicator.

7
Controlling Risk:
The Key to Profitability

Risk is inherent while trading in a dynamic, ever changing environment. And though there are many factors to risk, the result is always the same: unexpected losses to your trading account. This chapter will focus on some exciting new ways to control risk.

The main purpose for risk control is the use of leverage in trading futures, as leverage magnifies the adverse impact of market changes. Volatility is another reason to try to control risk: Markets now tend to make large moves very quickly, requiring even greater vigilance on your part. Of course, an obvious reason to control risks is to meet your profit objectives and margin requirements.

THE MENTAL STRESS OF TRADING

Still another, albeit implicit, reason for risk control is to fight the mental stress of trading. A series of big losses is enough to shake the confidence of most traders. The mathematics of losing is against you, too. For example, to recover from a 50 percent loss of initial capital, you need a 100 percent gain just to restore all your initial capital. Human psychology is such that winning is exhilarating, and losing is depressing. Even though, often, there are a few external reasons for both success and failure, they are hard to see regardless of whether we are winning or losing.

The trader also must bear the burden of working in a competitive, rapidly changing, and hostile environment in which many variables beyond your control can affect performance. The trader must also deal with the problem of information overload: A torrent of incomplete information vying for attention. Contrast this scenario to the slow moving, collegial world of an engineer designing a new product that will not go to market for another nine months. The engineer's world is usually well structured, with well defined goals and limited information sources. Couple that with the fact that the engineer is usually working within a team, which diffuses direct responsibility and, consequently, diffuses both blame and credit. The engineer's team also provides emotional support and serves as a network of resources. The trader, on the other hand, is flying solo: It's your trade, win or lose. The trader's peer group, on the other hand, is the competitor, which makes making trading a high-speed dogfight.

Within the trader's uncertain world, there is also the curse of hindsight. It is possible to look back upon yesterday or the day before and determine in an instant what should have been done. The same decisions, however, are more difficult to make in real time since you can't ever know for certain what the markets are going to do. Thus, trading demands intense concentration, which only heightens the emotional responses to winning and losing.

Another common cause of trading stress is what we call trend persistence, akin to persistence of vision. You can use the statistical test of runs to show that successive trades are independent events. However, as you trade in real time, your mind imposes trend persistence. It is easy to convince yourself that winning or losing streaks will persist, which causes mood swings between euphoria and depression or overconfidence and no confidence. Overconfidence can get you into bad trades, just as lack of confidence may keep you out of good ones.

There are no simple solutions for combatting any of these mental stresses, but a zealous approach to risk control is a large part of staying sane while you are in the game.

One way to sleep better at night is to minimize your theoretical risk of ruin, as discussed by Nauzer J. Balsara. Your trading success depends on the percentage of capital risked, the probability of success, the payoff ratio, and ultimately, on controlling risk.

ESTIMATING RISK ON NEW POSITIONS

The best place to begin risk control is to define the initial risk on every new position. You should have a clear idea of how much money you are willing to lose in each situation. Selecting this initial risk number should be your first step.

A good first estimate is the amount of the initial margin required to open the position. These margins change often, and your broker may require an amount greater than the exchange minimum margins. These margins are a measure of expected volatility, with the more volatile contracts usually requiring a larger margin. We recommend that your initial risk not exceed the required initial margin. A good choice is between 50 percent to 70 percent of initial margin.

Another way to select the initial risk number is as x percent of your current or initial account equity. We recommend using a number between 1–2.5 percent of the account. For example, if your initial equity is $150,000, you could use $1,500 as your initial risk.

A third way to select the initial risk is from the historical testing of your model. John Sweeney, the technical editor of *Stocks & Commodities* magazine suggests an approach called Maximum Adverse Excursion or MAE. He plots the worst loss or maximum adverse excursion for winning trades. In most useful systems, winning trades do not have MAE greater than an amount such as $1,000–$1,250 per contract. You should place your stop just beyond the worst loss shown by a majority of winning trades. If this dollar amount exceeds 2.5 percent of you equity, then set the stop at 2.5 percent.

Once you pick a number, you should place a stop loss order with your broker to close out the new position. It is essential that you maintain the loss control discipline by placing an order every day or one that is good for longer than a day. Your stop will get you out if the market moves against you.

Maximum Favorable Excursion

Sometimes you will see trades that start off profitably, but then quickly develop into losing positions. We call the measure of the best profit of an eventually losing trade the Maximum Favorable Excursion (MFE), the opposite of the MAE. If you analyze your winning and losing trades, you will find that the losing trades often showed a small profit during the course of the trade. The market then reversed and the trade ended at a loss. Similarly, winning trades usually went beyond the "small" profit and stayed there.

To get a better idea of how MAE and MFE work, look at data in Figure 7.1. This figure shows the MAE for profitable trades using a model for the British Pound. You'll see the result for 38 trades, of which 28 (74 percent) had a loss of less than $750; almost 90 percent of the trades had a worst loss of less than $1,000. Therefore, an initial money management stop of $1,050 would allow most profitable trades to continue. In addition, you must decide if this $1,050 limit also meets your risk exposure criterion: For example, you would like $1,000 to be less than, say, 2.5 percent of your equity.

To illustrate MFE, we show an analysis of losing trades for the same model in Figure 7.2. Out of 104 losing trades shown,

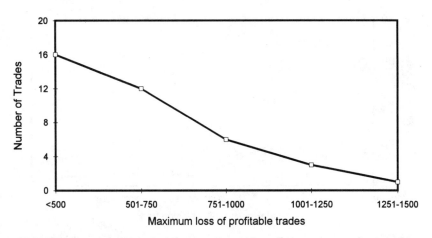

FIGURE 7.1   Maximum Adverse Excursion for a system that trades British Pound futures contract.

67 (64 percent) showed a maximum profit of less than $1,000. As many as 87 percent of the trades showed a maximum profit of less then $2,000. We surmise then that there is sufficient volatility in this market to stop us out even after a good profit. Thus, during trading, you must manage your stops aggressively when the profit is less than $2,000. You must try to avoid quick reversals that will stop you out at a loss. After the profit exceeds $2,000, the trade is likely to mature into a profitable one. Then you can move the stops to the breakeven point, and perhaps even loosen them a bit to prevent being stopped out by random fluctuations.

In short, MFE will help you manage trailing stops during the initial portion of the trade, when you are most likely to be stopped out.

Trailing Stops for Open Trades

Trailing stops can be used to protect open positions with a significant profit. The stop will get you out should the market

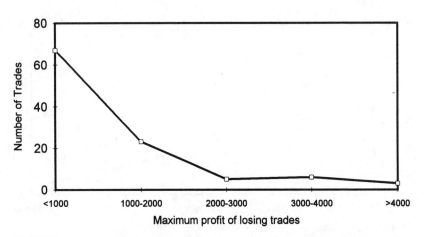

FIGURE 7.2   Maximum favorable excursion for a system that trades the British Pound futures contract.

make a sudden move against your position. The exact location of a stop is often critical to the outcome of the trade. Because of this, we'll discuss many different ways to set stops that you'll find useful at one point or another.

One of several methods for setting trailing stops is to change the stop just once a week. Say you use the Wednesday close to calculate the profit over the past week. You can then advance the stop x percent of the weekly profit, say 40 percent. This mechanical stop will advance when you have a profit, but will not step back when you have a weekly loss.

Another simple approach is to use a fixed dollar trailing stop. For instance, you could use a $1,500 trailing stop, measuring the amount from the highest high or lowest low during the trade. The exact dollar amount could be an arbitrary amount from $500 to $5,000 based on your trading style.

One classic method is to set the stop just below a swing low or high. A look at the price chart will show the most recent significant high or low. Though such a stop can be just beyond the recent high or low, be aware that such stops can be gunned by floor brokers.

You can set unique, difficult-to-gun stops, using VIDYA, as shown in Figure 7.3. Remember, VIDYA is a moving average that adapts to market volatility, which we discussed in Chapter 3. Since the moving average is based on closing prices, it does not account for the position of the most recent highest high or lowest low relative to today's close. Therefore, VIDYA stops are relatively "loose," and best used for long-term trades on a closing basis. Further, such stops may not protect open trade equity in volatile markets as effectively as the volatility-based stop discussed below.

Volatility-Based Trailing Stops

Volatility stops are another approach to setting smart stops that are not easily gunned. This approach is particularly useful for intermediate-term trades to prevent being shaken out by market turbulence. These stops are derived from the most recent highest high or lowest low, and they move farther away (loosen) from these extreme prices when volatility increases. The loosening of the stop, which prevents premature shak-

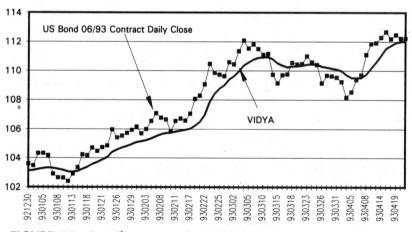

FIGURE 7.3 A trailing stop using VIDYA.

eout, also means that you must give up a sizeable chunk of your profit if the stop is hit. Our solution is to modify this approach in such a way that the stop can only advance with prices, not retreat. This will lock in a greater portion of potential profits, but still allow the market room to wiggle.

We begin by calculating a 10-day simple moving average of the average true range (ATR). This function is available in most technical analysis software. If it is not available, you can use the absolute daily closing changes over the last 10 days and average them instead. We'll call this quantity ATR_{10}. For long trades, subtract the amount ($3*ATR_{10}$) from the highest high over the last 10 days. We'll call this quantity our preliminary long stop. Finally, use the highest value of the preliminary stop over the last 20 days as the actual stop for long trades.

For short trades, add the amount ($3*ATR_{10}$) to the lowest low of the last 10 days, calling this quantity our preliminary short stop. Finally, use the lowest value of the preliminary short stop over the last 20 days as the actual stop for short trades.

You can experiment with the ATR_{10} multiplier to get a looser ($4*ATR_{10}$) or tighter ($2*ATR_{10}$) stop. Or, you can use a different time period to calculate the average of the ATR, or to calculate the highest (lowest) value of the preliminary stops.

Figure 7.4 shows a tight ($1.5*ATR_{10}$) and a loose ($3.5*ATR_{10}$) volatility stop for a long trade in the September, 1993 Japanese Yen contract. Note how the stops flattened out during volatile, sideways periods while advancing with rising prices. There are two ways to use these stops. As an intermediate-term trader, you could use the looser stop as the trailing stop. If this stop were hit intraday, you would use the tighter stop for reentering long trades. For instance, if you were stopped out in early May when prices touched the loose stop, you would have gone long when prices closed above the tighter stop. This would have provided an excellent reentry point.

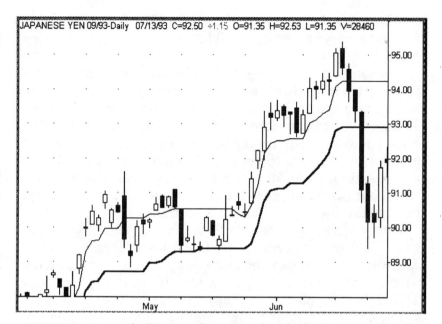

JAPANESE YEN 09/93-Daily 07/13/93 C=92.50 +1.15 O=91.35 H=92.53 L=91.35 V=28460

FIGURE 7.4   A volatility-based stop used with the Japanese Yen futures contract.

As a short-term trader, you would use the tighter stop on either an intraday or closing basis. Notice how the prices stayed above the tighter stop during strong up swings. As expected, the tighter stop would have exited the position sooner than the looser stop near the June highs. However, the tighter stops would have produced whipsaw trades during the price consolidation in April and May. Hence, your trading style would determine your choice of stops.

DEVELOPING A TRADE TEMPLATE

One of the toughest problems in managing the open trade is deciding when to take profits. Usually, there is no simple answer since you can encounter so many different market

conditions. We suggest that you use the historical trading performance of your system to plot a template for assessing
trades.

You can plot the day-by-day evolution of each trade from
your system by plotting the best and worst equity of each day
on separate charts. If your system has provided more than
30 trades, you can develop a fairly representative trade profile.
First, you would average the best equity of each trade on the
first day of the trade to get a single number for day 1. Then
you would do so for day 2 and so on. (There may be fewer
trades open as the number of days increases.) Then you would
average the equity across only open trades.

Your plot should be similar to the one shown in Figure 7.5,
which is from a system for trading 10-year Treasury notes.
The middle line shows the best equity for the average trade,
which peaks nine trading days into its existence at about
$1,500. We also plotted the lines one standard deviation (+1
sigma and −1 sigma) away on either side of the average.
These plots should account for about 67 percent of the trades
from this model. The upper line shows that the more prof-

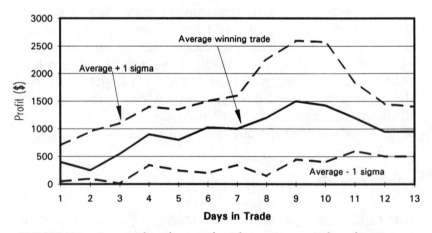

FIGURE 7.5   A typical trade template for a system trading the 10-year
Treasury Note contract.

itable trades peak 9–10 days from inception at an equity of $2,500. If the trade is moving slowly but is profitable, the lower line suggests it would peak at about 11 days with a profit barely above $500.

This plot now serves as a template suggesting how the trade may evolve in time and price. Using Figure 7.5, let's assume the market is strong and you had a $4,000 profit after just three days in the trade. We would urge you to take your profits, or at least, tighten your trailing stop since the template suggests the trade is ahead of itself. In contrast, if you had a $1,000 loss on day 4, we would suggest closing the trade since it seems unlikely to succeed.

We show the evolution of two trades in Figure 7.6 in which there is one big winner and an average trade. Note how the big winner's equity peaked at nine days as expected. The other trade peaked at 11 days. By showing the potential evolution of trades in price and time, a template gives you an estimate of the probable course of a trade. Actual trades may develop faster or slower, and could last longer. You can conclude from this that it's also important to check your reentry rules after exiting a trade using the template.

Just as the trade template is an anticipatory technique, you can use price projection methods to develop different scenarios for trade planning.

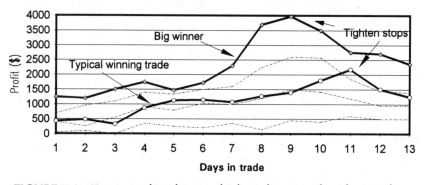

FIGURE 7.6   Two actual trades overlaid on the typical trade template for the 10-year Treasury Note contract.

ANTICIPATING PRICES FOR A RISK CONTROL PLAN

Thus far in this chapter we used passive risk control strategies, such as setting an initial risk or using different trailing stops. Implicitly, we assumed little about the next day's possible range of prices. The trade template anticipates prices in a general way, but does not explicitly account for the actual nature of recent market action.

In this section, we propose a more proactive approach toward risk control that is based on anticipating the possible range of prices for the next trading day. Since the anticipated range is only a guess, the trading plan develops specific actions for exit, entry, or reentry, whether the market trades inside or outside the expected range. In this sense, the plan looks at risk as well as reward.

Specifically, we will develop two target prices (H1 and H2) that are higher than today's close, and two target prices (L1 and L2) that are lower than today's close. L1 and L2 represent two levels of risk for a long position, and H1 and H2 are the two levels of reward. The reverse is true if we have a short position. Our goal is to develop specific orders to be entered under the following conditions during the next trading day:

- Price exceeds H2.
- Price trades between H2 and H1.
- Price trades between H1 and L1.
- Price trades between L1 and L2.
- Prices falls below L2.

In actual trading, literally thousands of different patterns could occur between the limits H2 and L2, and the possibilities just listed cover only a few situations. They are, however, a good starting point. First, though, let's discuss how to obtain the price targets.

First, you calculate the absolute daily difference between today's price and yesterday's price. Then, take a 10-day simple moving average of these daily differences. Note that this is similar to the ATR_{10} number used in volatility stop calculations. (In fact, you could use ATR_{10} if you wish.) We'll denote this average by the letter A, and project tomorrow's price range by adding some multiple of A to today's closing price, as shown in the following equations:

$$|\text{momentum}| = |C_0 - C_1|,$$
$$A = \text{10-day simple moving average of } |\text{momentum}|,$$
$$H1 = C_0 + A,$$
$$H2 = C_0 + 2*A, \qquad\qquad (7.1)$$
$$L1 = C_0 - A,$$
$$L2 = C_0 - 2*A.$$

We denote the absolute momentum by $|\text{momentum}|$, today's close by C_0, and yesterday's close by C_1. The estimates for tomorrow's highs and lows are H1, H2, L1, and L2. This calculation says our best estimate for tomorrow's close is today's close. The total range is four times A (4*A), being a span of 2*A on either side of the close. You can vary the number of days used in the calculations as well as the multiples used to project the span. This approach has the advantage that, as market volatility changes, the projected span will change as well.

Now that we know how to compute price targets, we'll illustrate how you can develop scenarios and risk control plans. Assume that the market has been trending lower and you have a short position. A strong rally tomorrow would close near or above H2. You also feel that such a strong rally probably signals a reversal of the downtrend. In such a situation, you could choose to put in a stop order to close out your short and go long a few ticks above H2. But, if the market traded between H2 and H1, you would hold the short position and do nothing. Similarly, you would continue to hold your short position if the market traded between L1 and L2. In addition, however, you feel only a selling climax could push the market below L2, so you could decide to cover your short position (but not go long) if the market traded below L2 at any point during the day.

You could use the price targets as entry points. For instance, L1 could be an entry point into an existing uptrend for long positions. Similarly, you could look for short entries near H1, with a stop at H2 or between H1 and H2.

Another application of the projected price targets is to visualize how the daily chart would look should the market close within the inner band or at any other point inside the projected range. Such a close might complete or start a price pattern that may have predictive value. In this way, you can get a jump on your chart analysis by using the projected range as a template for tomorrow's price bar.

These examples show that you can work out many different scenarios within objective projections of the next trading range. The important point to note is that you can identify specific price levels for concrete trading decisions.

How well do the projected price targets work? Figure 7.7 shows the projected price targets for the Japanese yen September, 1993 contract. Note how this market often found support and resistance near the inner bands (H1 and L1). The yen easily reached or exceeded the outer bands (H2 or L2) on strong up and down days, and found support and resistance at the outer bands at major turning points. You can see how the bands widened in response to the increasing volatility from early June to early July. Thus, the projected price targets would have been quite useful for developing a risk control plan.

The August, 1993 Comex Gold (Figure 7.8) contract provides another example from the futures markets. Gold often traded outside the (H1-L1) inner band. During the intermediate top in June, 1993, an open outside H2 was a good profit-taking opportunity as you may expect. The H1 band provided good entries for short trades in late May. Similarly, the L1 band provided good entries for long trades in June. This chart also shows how the bands narrow and widen in response to

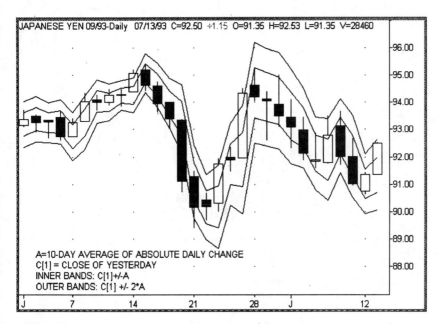

JAPANESE YEN 09/93-Daily   07/13/93 C=92.50 +1.15 O=91.35 H=92.53 L=91.35 V=28460

A=10-DAY AVERAGE OF ABSOLUTE DAILY CHANGE
C[1] = CLOSE OF YESTERDAY
INNER BANDS: C[1]+/-A
OUTER BANDS: C[1] +/- 2*A

FIGURE 7.7   The Japanese Yen September, 1993 contract is shown with the projected price targets.

changing volatility. This feature is useful in trading the volatile futures markets.

In sum, it is clear that our proactive risk control strategy based on projected price ranges can be successfully implemented in the futures markets.

PRACTICAL ISSUES IN RISK CONTROL

We have discussed a number of different approaches for risk control without touching upon some of the operational details of making them work. In this section, we'll mention a few items that may help you execute your risk control strategies more smoothly.

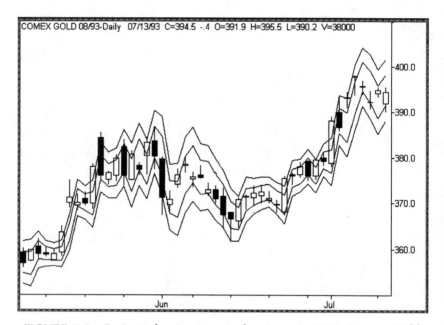

FIGURE 7.8 Projected price targets for August, 1993 Comex Gold contract.

When you develop your price targets H2, H1, L1, and L2, observe whether they fall near any significant retracement points such as 33 percent, 50 percent, or 67 percent for the current move. These are called Fibonacci retracements, and often provide points of support and resistance. Figure 7.9 shows these Fibonacci retracements in the High-Grade Copper September, 1993 contract. The major move from A to B produced a 50 percent retracement to C. Smaller moves from A to g produced a 64 percent retracement to h. Similarly, the move from d to f produced a 47 percent retracement to e. The conclusion? Pay particular attention if your projected targets happen to be near Fibonacci retracement levels.

After you calculate a trailing stop, avoid placing it near a round number such as 62.00 or 62.50, but place it 7-33 ticks past the round number. For example, set your sell stop at

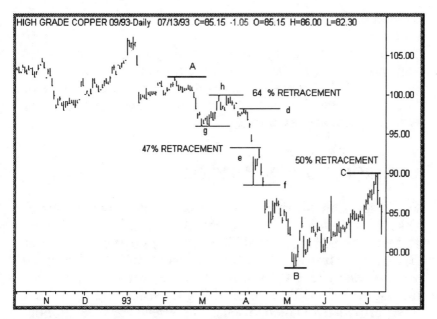

FIGURE 7.9 High Grade Copper September, 1993 contract showing Fibonacci retracements.

60.87 and hope that the market will find support near 61.00. You may notice that reversals in the US T-Bond market usually occur less than 7 ticks beyond the previous high or low. Therefore, try to place your stop say 11 ticks beyond the previous high or low. Often, those few extra ticks may be the difference between having a winning trade or avoiding a losing one.

Even though we have continually mentioned stops (stop orders) for risk control, using market orders may be the best way to exit a position during the trading day. Once you decide to close a position, get out as fast as possible.

Study the type of orders your broker will accept, since they can influence how you actually enter orders for your risk control plan. A well-placed order will help you trade better. Another order placement tactic is to use the facsimile machine to send orders, since it avoids confusion and simplifies error correction.

One final order entry tip: Next time you have to roll over your position in an expiring contract, use market orders, but on a "not-held" basis, giving your broker the discretion in filling your trades at a time when the spreads between the two contracts are favorable.

CONTROLLING "INVISIBLE" RISKS

Our discussion on risk control was oriented towards price-risk, but be aware that there are many other forms of risk, and you should recognize their existence as part of your larger risk control strategy. We call these risks "invisible," because you can easily lose sight of them in the heat of trading. Our discussion here will be brief, though, because other authors have provided detailed discussions elsewhere (see Bibliography).

Because many markets are correlated, you incur portfolio risk from the combination of markets you trade. Remember that trading correlated markets is equivalent to trading multiple contracts in a single market. Market characteristics such as gaps, volatility, liquidity, and order execution are other factors that influence risks arising from your portfolio. Diversification over six or more markets is one approach to controlling these risks.

Your asset allocation and use of leverage are other forms of risk. There are many ways to balance the amount of capital risked to trading with the desired risk-return tradeoffs. We refer you to the books by Nauzer J. Balsara and Ralph Vince for a discussion of these issues. Popular rules include risking 2.5 percent or less of total equity per trade, and using 30 percent or less of total equity toward margin requirements.

In short, you assume many "invisible" risks when trading today's markets. As a result, you should address these forms of risk as part of your overall risk control strategy.

8
How to Use This Book

The best way to use this book is to integrate our ideas into your own trading process. We'll give you examples of how it can be done by combining indicators to find new, effective trading systems. For instance, we'll show you how to develop an adaptive trading system combining the momentum oscillator, CMO, with VIDYA. We'll also show how you can use the ideas of composite momentum and linear regression analysis for market rotation—moving out of quiet markets into those experiencing major moves. We hope these examples may stimulate other ideas in your own mind on how to combine the new indicators in this book.

A CMO-DRIVEN VIDYA TRADING SYSTEM

The varying volatility of markets causes particular difficulty for long-term systems: They tend to generate more false signals. Obviously, then, a system that adapts to market volatility would be highly desirable for long-term trend following. Another significant advantage of an adaptive system versus fixed parameter systems is that you do not have to worry about optimizing system parameters. Optimized system parameters often work wonderfully on historical data, but fail miserably in real-time trading.

We will build our system using VIDYA, the adaptive moving average. We will index VIDYA to market momentum using the absolute Chande momentum oscillator (absCMO) as discussed in Chapter 3. Our CMO-driven VIDYA based system will attempt to follow long-term trends, perhaps with a winning percentage around 40 percent and a payoff ratio greater than 2.50.

We want to combine VIDYA and CMO in such a way that the effective length of the moving average increases when the market has low momentum (absCMO values near 0). Further, we want the effective length to decrease when the market gains momentum (absCMO > 0.30). Ideally, this average would move rapidly when prices make a big move. Then, as momentum slows, the average will slow down also.

To combine CMO and VIDYA, we'll first define CMO in terms of the unsmoothed 9-day RSI because we'll use the System Writer software from Omega Research for our calculations, which provides the unsmoothed RSI as a built-in function. We'll use that function to calculate CMO, dividing CMO by 100 to get numbers between +1 and −1, rather than +100 and −100. We arbitrarily used a 9-day RSI to calculate CMO of the daily close. Nine days is a popular choice for short-to-intermediate analysis, but, you could use a 14-day CMO or any other length you wish. Second, we will take the absolute value of CMO to eliminate the negative sign, and multiply it by a scaling constant t. This scaling constant t is less than or equal to 0.50 to provide a smooth conversion between CMO and VIDYA. We will designate the scaled, absolute CMO by the symbol A. Hence, the equations for calculating CMO and VIDYA are:

$$|CMO| = |(2*RSI_9 - 100)/100|,$$
$$A = t*|CMO| \ (t <= 0.5), \qquad (8.1)$$
$$VIDYA_d = A * Close + (1-A) * VIDYA_{d-1}.$$

When the market is trending strongly, VIDYA will have strong momentum in the trend's direction which will give high values of the absolute CMO. As A increases, the term A * Close in the definition of VIDYA increases. The average is then taking larger chunks out of new data, decreasing the effective length of the average. The opposite happens when momentum decreases during sideways periods.

To choose a value for the scaling constant t, we want to avoid testing over a variety of values to find one particular value that works best. Our design goal is for a long VIDYA, so a "small" value of t, such as 0.05, 0.10, 0.15, or 0.20, is what we really need. Equation 8.1 for VIDYA shows that as the values of t decrease, the term A also decreases, and we use smaller and smaller fractions of new data to update VIDYA, increasing the effective length of VIDYA. Now we can pick a value between 0.05 and 0.20 arbitrarily. Or, we can use additional calculations to help narrow the choice.

The approach we used to choose a value for t was to test the four values, 0.05, 0.10, 0.15, and 0.20 over 24 markets using the data from 01/01/92 to 04/26/93. We again used the CSI #39 Perpetual contract. The results are in the Table 8.1, with the columns showing net profit (or loss) for different values of t. On studying the average profit in Table 8.1 for different values of t, we found that the results were very similar for t=0.10 and t=0.15. Consequently, we decided to use the value t=0.1 as our constant across all markets and time periods.

When $|CMO| = 1$, t=0.1 translates into a 19-day exponential moving average, which meets our design criterion of using a long VIDYA. We can now define the long and short entry rules as follows:

1. *The rule to open long positions.* If the close of today and yesterday are both above the VIDYA of today, then buy tomorrow on a buy stop order. Place the order 1 tick above today's high.

2. *The rule to short positions.* If the close of today and the

Table 8.1 Effect of Changing Scaling Constant t

| | ← Scale t for VIDYA → | | | |
Market	0.05	0.10	0.15	0.20
Bean oil	−1078	302	−2778	−3598
British pound	16682	25706	31381	30537
Canadian $	1480	2230	2860	2860
Cocoa	−2170	−1930	−350	−2070
Coffee	11177	9005	5841	718
Cotton	−515	−5	−4530	−7310
Crude oil	−790	−150	−1490	−610
Deutsch mark	8000	5837	5087	3212
Eurodollars	1025	3125	3325	2525
Gold	−2350	2410	3250	5550
Heating oil	109	−1293	177	−2013
HG copper	4372	5082	4687	5787
Japanese yen	6887	10287	13412	14325
Live cattle	−1548	−2013	1312	820
Live hogs	4175	4716	5106	4900
Pork bellies	−5492	−3704	−163	−1306
Silver	−4955	−2890	−4115	−5075
Soybeans	3150	2213	2663	800
Sugar	2824	1091	2983	510
Swiss franc	15050	22463	21262	5775
T-note 10-yr	6481	11137	11918	8812
US bond	2981	6612	−1087	−6206
USDX	1920	5240	1470	1290
Wheat	2206	3032	5431	4043
Average	2785.04	4340.52	4306.68	2571.84
Stand. Dev	5529.34	7147.56	7987.04	7521.35
Avg/stdev	0.50	0.61	0.54	0.34
Max	16682	25706	31381	30537
Min	−5492	−3704	−4530	−7310
Max/min	3.04	6.94	6.93	4.18

close of yesterday are both below the VIDYA of today, then sell tomorrow on a sell stop order. Place the order 1 tick below today's low.

You also could trade on a closing basis for stocks and mutual funds. We won't use any specific exit strategy in testing the model, which means a long entry signal will exit a short trade and vice versa. We'll use a $1,500 initial stop, which can be refined later using the MAE or maximum adverse excursion idea. We'll increase losses by $125 and decrease profits by $125 to allow for slippage and commissions.

Our data comes from Commodity Systems Inc. (CSI), in the form of their #39 Perpetual Contract, though you can use any other perpetual contract or continuous data you like. We will use ten years of data for the Swiss franc contract starting 05/26/83 and use the System Writer Plus (SWP) software package for system testing. The data will be divided into two approximately equal five-year blocks. First we'll test the model over the May, 1983 to May, 1988 period. Then, we'll run it over the May, 1988 to April, 1993 period.

Remember, we are hoping our long-term model for the Swiss franc will have a winning percentage between 30–45 percent and a payoff ratio greater than 2.50. Let's see then how our expectation matches up with the results from the first five-year block, shown in Table 8.2. For starters, we know our test period was not too short since there were 33 trades over this test block. The SWP output shows that 36 percent of the trades were winners and the ratio of average winner/loser (payoff ratio) was 3.37; the payoff ratio was 3.18 without the largest winner and loser. On average, the model cut off losing trades in 13 trading days, and allowed the average winning trade to run 79 trading days. The average trade made a profit of more than $700, well above our slippage amount of $175. Thus, this unoptimized model did meet our main design goals from which we can conclude it is a reasonable long term trend following model.

An analysis of the MAE showed none of the winning trades

Table 8.2   Swiss Franc Test Block #1

Model Name	: Z New Vidya CMO Model
Notes	: Long Term CMO-based VIDYA model
Data	: SWISS FRANC CSI #39 Perpetual Contract
Calc Dates	: 05/26/83 – 05/30/88
Commissions	: $50
Slippage	: $75
Margin	: $3,000

Total net profit	$23,400.00
Gross profit	$48,662.50
Gross loss	$−25,262.50
Total # of trades	33
Percent profitable	36%
Number winning trades	12
Number losing trades	21
Largest winning trade	$8,262.50
Largest losing trade	$−2,175.00
Average winning trade	$4,055.21
Average losing trade	$−1,202.98
Ratio avg win/avg loss	3.37
Avg trade (win & loss)	$709.09
Max consecutive winners	2
Max consecutive losers	5
Avg # bars in winners	79
Avg # bars in losers	13
Max closed-out drawdown	$−5,950.00
Max intraday drawdown	$−6,850.00
Profit factor	1.92
Max # of contracts held	1
Account size required	$9,850.00
Return on account	237%

had an MAE of more than $1,000. Thus, in actual trading, we could use an initial money management stop of $1,050 instead of $1,500 used in the testing. Nevertheless, we will continue to use the $1,500 number when we test the model over the second data block to maintain consistency.

An analysis of the maximum favorable excursion (MFE) shows that:

- There were 12 losing trades with a maximum profit of less than $1,500.
- Another seven losing trades had a maximum profit of between $1,501 and $2,500.
- There were just two losing trades with a maximum profit of more than $2,500.

Thus, you could move your stop to the break-even point after a maximum profit of $2,501. You could also manage your stops more aggressively if the profit were more than $1,501.

Now that we have a model that worked on our first test block, we must do some "forward testing", that is, test it on another contiguous data block without changing any variables. This is called an "out-of-sample" test. The goal of the second set of tests is to check if the model performance degrades in any way. This might occur if we "curve-fitted" the model on the first set, by adding so many conditions that we picked up nuances in the test set that are unlikely to repeat in actual trading. The test over the second data block might tell us how well the model would do in real trading. If the performance were about the same on both blocks, we would have greater confidence in the model than if the performance were poor on the second set.

We next tested the Swiss franc data from 06/01/88 through 04/27/93; the results are in Table 8.3. We had 27 trades in this out-of-sample test, which we will generously round up to 30. Our results in this period were as good as the results in the first test period: Our winning percentage was the same

Table 8.3   Swiss Franc Test Block #2

Model Name	: Z New Vidya CMO model
Notes	: Out-of-sample test, long-term CMO-based VIDYA
Data	: SWISS FRANC CSI #39 Perpetual Contract
Calc Dates	: 06/01/88 – 04/27/93
Commission	: $50
Slippage	: $75
Margin	: $3,000

Total net profit	$49,775.00
Gross profit	$77,737.50
Gross loss	$−27,962.50
Total # of trades	27
Percent profitable	37%
Number winning trades	10
Number losing trades	17
Largest winning trade	$17,012.50
Largest losing trade	$−3,037.50
Average winning trade	$7,773.75
Average losing trade	$−1,644.85
Ratio avg win/avg loss	4.72
Avg trade (win & loss)	$1,843.52
Max consecutive winners	3
Max consecutive losers	4
Avg # bars in winners	102
Avg # bars in losers	10
Max closed-out drawdown	$−8,112.50
Max intra-day drawdown	
Profit factor	2.78
Max # of contracts held	1
Account size required	$11,712.50
Return on account	424%

(37 percent), and the payoff ratio was somewhat higher at 4.72. We recalculated the payoff ratio at 4.10 without the largest winning and losing trades. The average losing trade lasted about 10 trading days, with winning trades, on average, open for 102 trading days.

In all, our trend-following model did reasonably well over a 10-year time frame. Our 1988–93 test period had seven winning trades with an MAE less than $1,000, and 11 losing trades with an MFE less than $1,500. There were four losing trades with an MFE $1,501–$2,500 and only two losing trades with an MFE greater than $2,500. This shows that you could move up your stop to break even after a maximum profit of $2,501. The Swiss franc has sufficient volatility to knock out our initial stop before the model can give an opposite entry.

We also tested the model with continuous contracts developed using the Continuous Contractor software from TechTools over the same time period using CSI #39 Perpetual Contract. There was no significant difference in results with the two sets of data. We now had even more confidence in the model. A comparison for a four-year period is in Table 8.4.

As you can see, this model does follow long-term trends, judging by the number of trading days in the average winning trade. There are no guarantees that it will work as well in the future in every market, however. It is simply a good trend-following tool that adapts to market volatility, and it's probable that this model could be profitable in trending markets that have occasional volatile periods.

We could now test the model over successive 12-month periods to develop data on the variability in the payoff ratio and winning percentage. Or, for planning purposes, we could assume a 35 percent winning percentage and a payoff ratio of 2.50.

Two weaknesses in this model deserve mention. One is its performance in sideways markets or trendless markets that produce whipsaws. The other is its performance in very volatile markets, which can stop the trade out at a loss before

Table 8.4 Comparison: Perpetual Vs. Continuous Contract Data
Swiss Franc Contract

Model Name	: Z New Vidya CMO model
Notes	: Checks on CSI and Continuous Contract
Calc Dates	: 01/26/88 – 03/25/92
Commission	: $50
Slippage	: $75
Margin	: $3,000

Data :	CSI #39	Continuous Contract
Total net profit	$31,237.50	$29,737.50
Gross profit	$56,900.00	$57,912.50
Gross loss	$−25,662.00	$−28,175.00
Total # of trades	29	30
Percent profitable	27%	23%
Number winning trades	8	7
Number losing trades	21	23
Largest winning trade	$17,300.00	$17,312.50
Largest losing trade	$−2,900.00	$−2,900.00
Average winning trade	$7,112.50	$8,723.21
Average losing trade	$−1,222.02	$−1,225.00
Ratio avg win/avg loss	5.82	6.75
Avg trade (win & loss)	$1,077.16	$991.25
Max consecutive winners	3	3
Max consecutive losers	7	7
Avg # bars in winners	98	109
Avg # bars in losers	8	9
Max closed-out drawdown	$−8,687.50	$−8,637.50
Max intraday drawdown	$−9,275.00	$−9,225.00
Profit factor	2.21	2.05
Max # of contracts held	1	
Account size required	$12,275.00	$12,225.00
Return on account	254%	243%

the model can generate an opposite signal. The volatility in the fall, 1992 was a good example of a period in which this model did not do well, which is not surprising since the model must be made insensitive for long-term trend following. Markets that have long trading ranges also inevitably produce losses, though VIDYA does help improve performance in volatile and sideways markets over other moving averages.

You can test other variations of this model, such as increasing its sensitivity by using a value of t greater than 0.10. Or, you could select a time period shorter than nine days to calculate the CMO used to drive this model.

You can now proceed to integrate risk control with this model. For example, you could use VIDYA itself as a trailing stop, test a volatility-based stop as an exit strategy, rigorously testing each model. Be sure to review the results graphically to better understand model performance.

Before trading with the model, you could develop a typical trade template as discussed in Chapter 7 to understand trade evolution and consider discretionary exits. It should be apparent by now that the model calculations are only the starting point for building the complete system, which includes risk control and money management.

We hope this discussion has given you a feel for the process of developing a trend-following model that combines different indicators from the book. You'll probably agree that there are many tradeoffs and no one model can do it all.

MARKET ROTATION

Which markets should you be trading this week? The ones most likely to have big moves, of course, if you could identify them early enough. You'll find an answer to this eternal question if you use our new indicators to rank markets by their price action. You can then move out of inactive markets into active ones, a process we call market rotation, which is often the key to big profits in the ever-shifting futures markets.

Table 8.5 ranks 25 major futures markets on composite momentum and trendiness measures. Markets tend to stay near the top or bottom of the list for several days at a time, and hence market rotation provides significant trading opportunities. To rank markets, we found composite momentum, which was the sum of 5-day, 10-day, and 20-day momentum converted into dollars. We also found the 18-day slope and converted it into dollars. This shows the expected change in the daily close from a best-fit line.

There are two measures of trendiness: the 18-day r^2 of the best-fit line and the 18-day ADX. The trend was significant only if value of r^2 was greater than 0.22.

Table 8.5 shows the markets with the strongest uptrends near the top of the rankings; the markets with strong downtrends are near the bottom. The markets at the top or bottom may be surging, and good candidates for short-term trades. The markets in the middle are changing markets, and good candidates for new trading ideas. Because these markets may be consolidating within long-term trends, they may provide good entry points in the direction of the long-term trend. Further, since some of these markets may be seeing a change in the long term trend, they may be good candidates for taking antitrend positions or early positions in the direction of the new trend.

Table 8.5 presents a systematic method of surveying market trends and observing changes in trends. If you are a discretionary trader, you can rotate into markets that are strong. A systems trader could reject a signal from a trend-following model if the market is not trending. Or, you can wait for the trendiness indicators to strengthen before taking a new signal from a trend-following model. We have observed that markets stay near the top or bottom for many days at a time. Thus, these rankings are relatively stable from time to time, providing excellent opportunities for market rotation.

Some of you have probably guessed that the idea of market rotation could be generalized to stock rotation. Table 8.6 shows just such a sample stock trading list where we have

Table 8.5 Ranking Markets by Momentum Using Nearby Contract
(Data at close of: 04/29/92)

Market	Composite Momentum ($)	Slope 18-Day ($)	R-Sqd 18-Day	ADX 18-Day
Swiss franc	8288	232	0.74	48.72
British Pound	7550	234	0.73	54.67
Silver	6875	97	0.60	34.94
Coffee	6131	98	0.29	30.61
Gold	5340	97	0.67	45.89
Japanese yen	4738	205	0.63	40.61
Deutsche mark	4525	99	0.49	41.72
Sugar	3069	91	0.41	18.22
Cattle	1092	12	0.09	31.33
Heating oil	916	−17	0.26	12.00
Crude oil	530	−23	0.44	18.44
Eurodollar	94	60	0.28	25.22
Cocoa	−190	−3	0.01	14.33
Soybeans	−338	−14	0.20	22.06
Frozen OJ	−645	−68	0.61	28.17
Corn	−938	−28	0.67	45.00
Hogs	−1497	−40	0.62	21.11
Cotton	−1560	−51	0.39	15.28
Wheat	−1875	−48	0.76	34.78
US bond	−1906	74	0.11	26.33
Canadian $	−2180	−24	0.15	17.94
Copper	−4763	−152	0.73	64.83
US $ index	−6350	−181	0.77	51.44
Bellies	−8496	−138	0.56	11.78
Lumber	−14850	−173	0.26	56.33

Composite Momentum: Sum of 5-, 10- and 20-day momentum in dollars.
Slope: Slope of 18-day regression in dollars.
R-sqd: R-squared; trend exists if R-squared > 0.22.
ADX: Average Directional Index; trend exists if this is moving up and is greater than 0.20.

Table 8.6 Stocks: Ranked by Composite CMO   07/13/93

Rank	Stock	Com-posite	CMO10	CMO20	CMO30	CMO50
1	Tuscon Elec Pwr	39.30	33.33	37.50	14.81	41.94
2	Mexico Fund	37.12	55.56	42.22	10.38	19.57
3	Laidlaw B	32.48	46.15	46.84	6.90	16.22
4	Texas Utilities	24.36	47.83	41.46	1.62	3.28
5	Hansen Plc	15.95	63.64	12.50	−1.34	−8.33
6	South Wstrn Bell	14.89	37.93	5.66	3.60	5.17
7	BioTechGeneral	13.96	18.18	8.11	4.67	15.53
8	GTE	13.65	4.76	21.95	7.40	5.66
9	US Surgical	3.58	24.14	20.63	−6.96	−9.59
10	Philip Morris	−1.56	0.00	−4.62	−3.21	7.98
11	Bristol Myrs Sqb	−1.95	12.50	−10.59	−1.97	−3.81
12	Illinois Pwr Co	−2.17	−36.84	15.15	2.32	6.02
13	Nevada Power	−2.90	−14.29	7.69	−1.67	0.00
14	Mellon Bank	−3.53	−30.30	8.94	1.68	2.19
15	Amer Home Prod	−8.26	−1.96	−12.62	−3.66	−7.50
16	Abbot Labs	−9.49	−7.14	−8.20	−3.79	−11.27
17	Heinz	−12.16	−8.11	−18.64	−6.67	−1.89
18	Amgen	−13.25	−41.67	3.23	−.43	−13.29
19	Boeing	−15.56	−10.00	−24.44	−8.22	−3.17
20	Illinois Pwr Co	−19.15	−42.86	−17.81	−5.13	−.56
21	Varity	−19.41	−14.29	−23.33	−7.74	−16.83
22	Johnson & Johnson	−20.47	−12.82	−34.69	−8.21	−9.76
23	Pfizer	−24.09	−31.25	−34.94	−7.79	−6.81
24	Waste Mgmt	−24.18	−37.78	−36.08	−6.37	−3.78
25	Gap Stores	−27.96	−49.02	−28.74	−10.97	−1.22
26	Pepsi	−28.23	−65.22	−20.00	−4.53	−14.10
27	Merck	−29.40	−33.33	−47.37	−9.10	−9.62
28	Hong Kong Telcm	−33.96	−73.91	−29.63	−11.12	1.02
29	Laidlaw B	−45.74	−66.67	−52.38	−13.14	−24.53
30	Chemical Waste	−55.56	−53.85	−77.27	−18.53	−35.56

Rank = Ranked by average of all CMO values
CMO10 = 10-day Chande momentum oscillator
CMO20 = 20-day CMO
CMO30 = 30-day CMO
CMO50 = 50-day CMO
Composite = (CMO10 + CMO20 + CMO30 + CMO50)/4
Overbought at CMO >= 50
Oversold at CMO <= −50

ranked the stocks by a composite CMO. We first calculated the 10-, 20-, 30-, and 50-day Chande momentum oscillator, and used a simple arithmetic average of these values to rank the stocks. You would short the weakest stocks and buy the strongest. If you owned these stocks, you would tighten stops as the stocks weakened.

We calculated these rankings using daily data. If you wish, you can use weekly data for the rankings, which would reduce the frequency of trades since you would buy only those stocks with a positive CMO.

You also can use this ranking for antitrend trading by looking for overvalued stocks near the top of the rankings and undervalued stocks near the bottom. You also can look for a bounce in oversold stocks and a correction in overbought stocks. Table 8.6 includes four time periods, so you can study the numbers to see where each stock is in different time frames. Such a tally sheet is particularly useful when you study it for several weeks in a row. What's more, it's faster than reviewing the equivalent charts.

Let's review the "rotation" tables: We built them by combining the new indicators from momentum oscillators and linear regression. We also used the idea of combining data from different time intervals into a composite indicator. It should be apparent now how combining our ideas can improve your trading.

To further stimulate your creative processes, Table 8.7 shows how our indicators may be combined to gain an edge under different trading styles. You have already seen the detailed discussion of CMO-driven VIDYA and market rotation. One combination for stock market timing could combine Qstick, the StochRSI, the thrust oscillator, and price targets. For instance, you could take profits at the L1 price target if oversold conditions on Qstick and StochRSI are confirmed by extremes in the thrust oscillator. Here we combined intraday momentum (Qstick), with interday momentum (stochRSI), and advance/decline data (thrust oscillator). Tools for open trade management include the MFE, volatility

Table 8.7   Examples of Combining Indicators for Analysis

Item	CMO-driven VIDYA	Market Rotation	Stock Market Timing	Open Trade Management	Price Extremes	Trend-iness
Slope		*			*	
r²		*				*
VIDYA	*			*		
Qstick		*				
CMO	*	*			*	*
StochRSI			*		*	
MT			*			
Thrust Osc. (TO)			*			
MFE				*		
Volatility stop	*			*		*
Price Targets				*		
Trade template	*			*		

stop, price projection, and the trade template. They can help you place unique stops critical to profitability.

Depending on your time frame, you could identify price extremes using the regression slope or momentum oscillators (CMO, stochRSI, or DMI). On occasion, you may want to determine presence or absence of trendiness in a market by using the linear regression r², the absCMO, or even a volatility stop. You could derive many other combinations by adapting these flexible and powerful indicators to your trading style. We encourage you to do so, for your unique combination could boost your profits by giving you a much needed analytical edge in today's tough markets.

Bibliography

Altman, Roger. "Relative Momentum Index: Modifying RSI." *Technical Analysis of Stocks & Commodities*, Vol. 11, February, 1993 p. 30–35.

Arms, Richard. *The Arms Index: An Introduction to the Volume Analysis of the Stock and Bond Markets*. Homewood, IL: Dow Jones-Irwin, 1989.

Babcock Jr., Bruce. *Business One Irwin Guide to Trading Systems*. Homewood, IL:, Business One Irwin, 1989.

Balsara, Nauzer J. *Money Management Strategies for Futures Traders*. New York: John Wiley & Sons, Inc., 1992.

Blau, William. "The True Strength Index," *Technical Analysis of Stocks & Commodities*, Vol. 9 No. 11, November, 1991 pp. 18–31.

Burke, Gibbons, "Gain without Pain: Money Management in Action," *Futures*, Dec 1992, (Vol XXI #14) pp. 36–38.

Chande, Tushar S. "Adapting Moving Averages to Market Volatility." *Technical Analysis of Stocks & Commodities*, Vol. 10, No. 3 (Mar 1992), pp. 108–114. Copyright 1992 Technical Analysis, Inc. Used with permission.

Chande, Tushar S. "Forecasting Tomorrow's Trading Day." *Technical Analysis of Stocks & Commodities*. Vol. 10, No. 5 (May 1992), pp. 220–223. Copyright 1992 Technical Analysis, Inc. Used with permission.

Chande, Tushar S. "Market Thrust." *Technical Analysis of Stocks &*

Commodities. Vol. 10, No. 8 (Aug 1992), pp. 347–350. Copyright 1992 Technical Analysis, Inc. Used with permission.

Chande, Tushar S. "Smart Stops." *Technical Analysis of Stocks & Commodities.* Vol. 10, No. 12 (Dec 1992), pp. 507–509. Copyright 1992 Technical Analysis, Inc. Used with permission.

Chande, Tushar S., and Stanley Kroll. "Stochastic RSI and Dynamic Momentum Index." *Technical Analysis of Stocks & Commodities.* Vol. 11, No. 5 (May 1993). Copyright 1993 Technical Analysis, Inc. Used with permission.

Kaufman, Perry J. *The New Commodity Trading Systems and Methods.* New York: John Wiley & Sons, Inc., 1987.

Knight, Sheldon, "Tips, Tricks, and Tactics for Developing Trading Systems." *Futures,* Jan 1993 (Vol. XII, #1), pp. 38–40.

Knight, Sheldon. "Trading System Redux." *Futures,* Feb 1993 (Vol. XII, #2), pp. 34–36.

Kroll, Stanley. *Kroll on Futures Trading Strategy.* Homewood, IL: Dow Jones-Irwin, 1988.

Kroll, Stanley and Michael J. Paulenoff. *The Business One Guide to The Futures Markets.* Homewood, IL: Business One Irwin, 1993.

Le Beau, Charles and David W. Lucas. *Technical Traders Guide to Computer Analysis of the Futures Markets.* Homewood, IL: Business One Irwin, 1992.

Meibuhr, Stuart. "OEX and the Thrust Oscillator." *Technical Analysis of Stocks & Commodities.* March, 1993, p. 58.

Morris, Gregory. *Candlepower.* Chicago: Probus Publishing, 1993.

Murphy, John J. *Technical Analysis of the Futures Markets.* New York: New York Institute of Finance, 1986.

Nison, Steve. *Japanese Candlestick Forecasting Techniques.* New York: New York Institute of Finance, 1991.

Pardo, Robert. *Design, Testing, and Optimization of Trading Systems.* New York: John Wiley & Sons, Inc., 1992.

Schwager, Jack D. *A Complete Guide to the Futures Markets.* New York: John Wiley & Sons, Inc., 1984.

Snedecor, George W., and William G. Cochran. *Statistical Methods 8th Ed.* Ames, IA: Iowa State University Press, 1989.

Sweeney, John. "Where to Put Your Stops," *Technical Analysis of Stocks & Commodities.* December, 1992 (Vol 10, #13), p. 30.

Rotella, Robert P. *The Elements of Successful Trading.* New York: New York Institute of Finance, 1992.

Vince, Ralph. *The Mathematics of Money Management.* New York: John Wiley & Sons, Inc., 1992.

Vince, Ralph. *Portfolio Management Formulas.* New York: John Wiley
& Sons, Inc., 1990.
White, Adam. "Tuning into Trendiness with the VHF Indicator," *Futures*, Aug. 1991, p. 20–23.
Wilder Jr., J. Wells. *New Concepts in Technical Trading Systems.*
Greensboro, NC: Trend Research, 1978.

Index

A

Advancing Issues (AI), 143–45
Advancing Volume (AV), 143–45
Amgen (AMGN), 85–87, 130–31
Analysis of Variance (ANOVA)
   Table, 45
Antitrend Trading
   and dynamic momentum
      index (DMI), 134, 137, 140
   in futures markets, 190
   and linear regression analysis,
      25, 28
   and StochRSI measures, 124
   and stock rotation, 193
   and VIDYA bands, 54, 68
Arms, Richard, 144
Arms Index, ix, 144
   See also TRIN
Average Directional Index
(ADX)
   and Chande momentum
      oscillator (CMO), 108–10
   and dynamic momentum
      index (DMI), 140

and futures markets, 190
   and linear regression analysis,
      29–34
Average True Range (ATR), 168

B

Balsara, Nauzer J., 163, 178
Blau, William, 108
British Pound Futures, 164–65,
   166

C

Candlestick Analysis, 73–75
   and quantifying candlestick
      shadows, 82–84, 90
   See also Quantitative
      candlestick
Chande Momentum Oscillator
   (CMO), 11
   features of, 108–14, 118

CMO (*Continued*)
  filtering trade noise from,
    115–18, 141
  and relative strength index
    (RSI), 94–95, 141, 180
  and S&P-500 index, 97–106
  and stock rotation, 192–94
  and treasury bonds, 95–97,
    109–18
  and trendiness, 104–7, 140
  and VIDYA, 58, 60–62, 68–70,
    179–89
  and wheat futures, 108–9
Clinton, Bill, 65
Coffee Futures, 25–28, 79–81
Commodity Channel Index
    (CCI)
  limitations of, 93–94
  and similarities among
    indicators, 3, 5–7, 16–17
Commodity Systems, Inc. (CSI),
    7, 9, 25–27, 181–83, 187
Competition, 162
Contingency Planning, 13–14,
    39–40
Copper Futures, 176–77
Cotton Futures, 74

D

Declining Issues (DI), 143–45
Declining Volume (DV), 143–45
Deutsche Mark Contracts, 81,
    83–84, 90–91
Directional Movement System,
    3
Dow Jones Industrial Average
  and dynamic momentum
    index (DMI), 136–37

and thrust oscillator, 151–58
  See also Stock market
Dynamic Momentum Index
    (DMI), 12
  and Dow Jones Industrial
    Average, 136–37
  and S&P-500 index, 137–39
  trading strategies with, 140–41
  and volatility, 134–36, 141

E

Engineers, 162

F

Failure Rates of Indicators, 1–3
Fibonacci Retracements, 176
Flexible Parameter Trading
    Models, 137
Forecast Oscillator, 40–42

G

General Electric (GE), 87–89,
    107
Gold Futures, 20–23, 174–76

I

Intel Corporation (INTC), 29–34
Intraday Momentum Index
    (IMI), 80–81, 91–92
Interday trading
  See Stochastic RSI Oscillator
    and hourly data trading

J

Japanese Yen Futures, 168–69,
174–75

L

Leverage, 161, 178
Linear Regression Analysis, ix
and coffee futures, 25–28
and correlation among
indicators, 7–9
and dynamic momentum
index (DMI), 140
and Intel Corporation stock,
29–34
and market rotation, 179, 190,
193–94
and price forecasts, 10, 20,
34–42
and trendiness, 106
tutorial, 43–48
use of, 19–25, 43–48
and VIDYA, 60–63, 70–72
weaknesses in, 34

M

Market Rotation, 179, 189–94
Market Thrust, ix
compared to thrust oscillator
and TRIN, 149–50
defined, 145–49
and stock market advance
decline data, 12
Maximum Adverse Excursion
(MAE)
and risk control, 163–64

and setting stops, 183–85, 187
Maximum Favorable Excursion
(MFE)
and losing trades, x, 13
and risk control, 164–65
and setting stops, 185, 187,
193
Momentum Oscillators, ix
defined, 93
limitations of, 93–94
and rotation tables, 193
and VIDYA, 49
See also Chande momentum
oscillator (CMO)
Moving Average Convergence-
Divergence (MACD)
and similarities among
indicators, 5–6, 9, 17
and VIDYA, 54

N

New Concepts in Technical
Trading Systems (Wilder),
97
Noise Filters, 115–18, 131, 141

P

Philip Morris Stock, 4–9, 89
Plus Directional Movement
(DX+), 5, 16
Price Oscillator, 5, 7–8, 17
Price Patterns, 17–18
and limitations of momentum
oscillators, 93
and risk control plans, 174
Price Targets, x

Price Targets (*Continued*)
  and linear regression analysis,
    20
  and risk control plans, 172–76
  and stock market timing, 193

Q

Quantitative Candlestick
    (Qstick)
  calculation of, 90–91
  defined, ix, 11
  and momentum, 75–77, 79–
    81, 90
  and 1987 crash, 77–79, 87
  and stock prices, 85–89, 193
  and trading strategies, 76–77,
    84
  tutorial, 90–92

R

Random Prices, Generating of
  tutorial, 17–18
Relative Strength Index (RSI)
  and Amgen stock prices,
    130–31
  and Chande momentum
    oscillator (CMO), 94–95,
    141, 180
  and correlation among
    indicators, 9
  defined, 119–23
  and Dow Jones Industrial
    Average, 136–37
  and dynamic momentum
    index (DMI), 134–36, 141
  and intraday momentum
    index (IMI), 80–81

  limitations of, 11–12, 93–94
  and S&P-500 index, 97–104,
    127–30, 137–38
  and similarities among
    indicators, 3–6, 15–16
  static nature of, 49
  and stochastic oscillator, 124–
    33, 141, 193
  and thrust oscillator, 158
  and treasury bonds, 125–27,
    131–33
  tutorial, 119–23
  and VIDYA, 58
  and wheat futures, 108–9
Resistance
  and candlestick analysis,
    83–84
  and price changes, 2–3
  and VIDYA bands, 54, 63
Risk Control
  and anticipating prices, 3,
    172–76
  and correlated markets, 178
  and estimates on new
    positions, 163–69
  and leverage, 161, 178
  and linear regression analysis,
    35
  and mental stress, 161–63
  and trade templates, 169–72,
    189
  and VIDYA, 58, 189

S

S&P-500 Index
  and Chande momentum
    oscillator (CMO), 104–6

and dynamic momentum
index (DMI), 137–39
and relative strength index
(RSI), 97–103, 119–21
and StochRSI, 127–30
and thrust oscillator, 156
Stochastic Oscillator
and correlation among
indicators, 9
limitations of, 93–94
and relative strength index
(RSI), 124–33, 141, 193
and similarities among
indicators, 3–6, 15–16
Stochastic RSI Oscillator
(Stoch RSI), 124–33
and hourly data (intraday)
trading, 131–33
and RSI and the T-bond
market, 125
and S&P-500 index, 127–30
and trading strategies, 130–33
Stock Market
analyzing advances and
declines in, 143–45
and market thrust, 12
and 1987 crash, 77–79, 87
and Qstick analysis, 85–89
and stock rotation, 190,
192–93
See also Dow Jones Industrial
Average
Stops, Setting of
and candlestick analysis, 84
and linear regression analysis,
25, 35, 40
and maximum adverse
excursion (MAE), 164, 185
and maximum favorable
excursion (MFE), 165, 185,
187

and price targets, 173
and stock rotation, 193
and trailing stops for open
trades, 165–71, 176–77, 189,
193–94
and VIDYA, 54, 55, 58, 62,
63, 68, 167, 181, 183
Stress, 161–63
Support
and candlestick analysis,
83–84
and price changes, 2–3
and VIDYA bands, 54, 63
Sweeney, John, 163
Swiss Franc Futures, 183–89

T

Thrust Oscillator, 12
compared to market thrust
and TRIN, 149–50, 159
defined, 145–49
and Dow Jones Industrial
Average, 150–58
and S&P-500 index, 156
trading strategies with, 156–
58, 193
Trade Template, 169–72, 189,
194
Trading Bands
and candlestick analysis, 74
and VIDYA, 54–55, 58–59, 63,
67–68
Treasury Bonds
and candlestick analysis,
82–83
and Chande momentum
oscillator (CMO), 95–97,
109–18

Treasury Bonds (*Continued*)
  forecasts for, 34–42
  and relative strength index
    (RSI), 125–27, 131–33
  setting stops for, 177
  and VIDYA, 55–62, 63–72
Treasury Notes, 170–71
TRIN, 12
  and Dow Jones Industrial
    Average, 151, 153–56
  and thrust oscillator, 144–47,
    149–50, 159
True Strength Index (TSI),
  108–9
Tutorials
  on linear regression analysis,
    43–48
  on Qstick, 90–92
  on Random prices, generating
    of, 17–18
  on RSI, defining, 119–123
  on spreadsheets for VIDYA,
    63–72

V

Variable Index Dynamic Average
  (VIDYA)
  and advantages over static
    indicators, 49
  calculation of, 63–72
  and Chande momentum
    oscillator (CMO), 11–12, 58,
    60–63, 68–70, 179–89
  defined, ix, 11
  dynamic range of, 52–54, 63

and linear regression analysis,
  60–63, 70–72
  and trading strategies, 54–55,
    58, 63, 66, 68
  and trailing stops, 167
  and treasury bond market
    analysis, 55–62, 63–72
  tutorial, 63–72
  and volatility, 51–52, 54, 55,
    58, 63–65, 67–68
Variable Length Moving
  Average, 10–11
  See also VIDYA
Vertical Horizontal Filter
  (VHF), 29–34, 104–7
VIDYA
  See Variable Index Dynamic
    Average
Vince, Ralph, 178
Volatility Index
  and assessing price action, 51–
    52, 63–64
  and dynamic momentum
    index (DMI), 135, 141

W

Wheat Futures, 108–9
Whipsaw Trades, 130, 169, 187
White, Adam, 33
Wilder, J. Welles, Jr., 29
  and calculation of relative
    strength index (RSI), 97,
    121, 122–23
William's %R
  See Stochastic oscillator